Dave Tomlinson is Vicar of St Lu
North London. He set up and for t
unconventional church group meet   .... pub. He
holds a Masters degree in biblical interpretation, and wrote
The Post-Evangelical (also published by SPCK). He is married with three children and three grandchildren.

To all my friends at St Luke's, West Holloway

Running into God

Reflections for Ordinary Days

Dave Tomlinson

First published in Great Britain in 2004 by
Society for Promoting Christian Knowledge
36 Causton Street
London SW1P 4AU

Unless otherwise noted, the Scripture quotations contained herein
are from the New Revised Standard Version of the Bible:
Anglicized Edition, copyright © 1989, 1995 by the Division
of Christian Education of the National Council of the Churches
of Christ in the United States of America, and are used by
permission. All rights reserved.

Extracts from the New English Bible © Oxford University Press
and Cambridge University Press, 1961, 1970.

Extracts from *The Alternative Service Book 1980* and
Common Worship are copyright © the Archbishops' Council
and are reproduced by permission.

pp. 8–10, lines from "Christmas" by John Betjeman, reproduced
by permission of John Murray Publishers.

pp. 63–4, lines from *Letters to a Young Poet* by Rainer Maria
Rilke, translated by Stephen Mitchell, copyright © 1984 by
Stephen Mitchell. Used by permission of Random House, Inc.

SPCK does not necessarily endorse the individual views
contained in its publications.

British Library Cataloguing-in-Publication Data
A catalogue record for this book is available from
the British Library

ISBN 0–281–05695–1

1 3 5 7 9 10 8 6 4 2

Typeset by Avocet Typeset, Chilton, Aylesbury, Bucks
Printed in Great Britain by Bookmarque Ltd, Croydon, Surrey

Contents

Acknowledgements

Throughout my life I have 'run into God' in many people and situations, but nowhere have I encountered him more than in the ordinary everyday life of my family. Pat is far more than a wife to me; she is a true partner in everything I do. The people at St Luke's know that when I became their vicar they also acquired a talented and untiring manager of church affairs – someone who is everything I am not! Pat has always been my best critic, inspirer and editor of ideas. I thank her for the work she did in scrutinizing the proofs of this book – and for being the unrecognized voice in so much that I say.

Similarly, I owe a great debt to our three children, Jeni, Paul and Lissie, and their respective partners. For 35 years they have helped shape and fashion my ordinariness. My ministry as a speaker and writer is what it is because of their love and friendship.

In 1989 I decided to leave behind 20 years of work and ministry in the House Churches. I did so having no idea what would come next or where, if anywhere, my particular gifts should be exercised in the Church. I would like to thank Richard Chartres, the Bishop of London, for his encouragement and for his vision for me in the Church of England – the weird and wonderful family to which I have become so attached. My ordination in 1997 has led to the most satisfying stage of my life and ministry so far.

Many thanks to Stuart and Laura who, along with Pat, came up with the idea that this material should be turned into a book. It is not a book I simply sat down and wrote. It was penned over two years, bit by bit, without any realization that it would fit together as one volume. Each chapter started its life as a Sunday morning talk at St Luke's, West Holloway (www.saintlukeschurch.org.uk). I cannot think of another church where I would rather be the vicar. The people of St Luke's are my friends and companions on an exciting journey, and I thank them so much for all that they contribute to my life week by week. This book really would not exist apart from them.

Last but not least, I am grateful to all the staff at SPCK and to Alison Barr in particular for her help and encouragement with this and other writings. And thank you to Sally Green, Kathryn Wolfendale and Jo Bramwell for their work in knocking the book into shape.

Introduction

Not having grown up in a church with a liturgical tradition, my appreciation of the church calendar has come later in life. Of course I have always celebrated the great festivals like Christmas and Easter, but I never managed to fit them into the whole cycle of seasons, which I have now come to love so much.

One of the great strengths of the liturgical year, in the northern hemisphere at least, is the way it interacts with the natural seasons. This means that the differing shades of human experience symbolized in the seasons of nature are all given their place in the cycle of church worship. So, we do not need to pretend that Christian spirituality leads to constant feelings of summery cheerfulness: in the autumn, for example, we reconnect with feelings of grief and loss through the season of remembrance in All Saints and All Souls; during Lent we confront our own inner demons and recommit ourselves to Christ and his kingdom; and in Advent we journey through darkness in search of light and hope.

However, what I did not realize about the church calendar until I was ordained is that the majority of the year is simply designated as 'ordinary' time. The idea of ordinary time really appeals to me. After all, life itself is mostly ordinary, and I for one am pretty happy with that arrangement. Don't get me wrong, I love the special bits of life as much as anyone – holidays, birthdays, visits from friends, etc. – but there is something reassuring about returning home after a holiday or resuming one's normal routine after the visitors have left. Apart from anything else, special times would hardly be special if they occurred too frequently. It would be like having a five-course dinner party every evening: before long we would long for sausage and mash, fish and chips or beans on toast.

I often think it is sad that people who only attend church very rarely tend to turn up at Christmas, or Easter, or on special occasions like weddings or baptisms. The rich diet served up at such times hardly offers the sustenance required for day-to-day spiritual well-being. If only people would just decide to appear on the second before Lent, or the sixteenth after Trinity – just an ordinary Sunday. The tingles down the spine felt at Midnight Mass, or the warm glow experienced when two friends blushingly say their wedding vows in front of a packed church are indeed moments not to be missed, but the place we really need to discover God is in the midst of life's ordinariness.

The reflections in this book represent a wide spectrum of life's experiences; they are based on talks I gave at St Luke's throughout the church year. Some do indeed focus on the feasts, festivals and special seasons, but the vast majority are reflections for ordinary days.

Actually, it was only when I started to compile the book that I realised just how pervasive the theme of 'ordinariness' is in my thinking. I believe in a God of the ordinary, a God who inhabits ordinary people and ordinary situations. Nowhere is this revealed more demonstratively than in the Eucharist, where ordinary bread and wine, consecrated through prayer, become the bearers of divine grace. The Offertory prayer makes the point so eloquently:

Blessed are you, Lord God of all creation,
through your goodness we have these gifts to offer
which earth has given and human hands have made;
they will become for us the bread of life
and the cup of salvation.
Blessed be God for ever.

Basically, this book is an affirmation of the sacrament of ordinariness – a belief that we are likely to run into God anywhere, any time, in any situation, through any person or being. Be sure to keep an eye out for him, won't you?

Entering the circle

Psalm 25.1–10, Luke 21.25–36

A couple of weeks ago Vikki called me to say that she was planning to create our Advent and Christmas decorations around the theme of wreaths. And being the deeply thoughtful woman she is, she wanted to check out the theology of wreaths. So she called me to ask for my advice. Well, not wishing to appear a smart Alec – and never having given the subject a moment's consideration – I asked her what she thought. And as you can imagine, she came up with an excellent answer: that the wreath symbolizes God's unending love. So I said, 'That sounds good enough for me, Vikki.'

Of course, like so many Christian symbols, the wreath has its roots in paganism. Its origins are actually found in the folk practices of the pre-Christian Germanic peoples who, during the cold December darkness of Eastern Europe, gathered wreaths of evergreen, and lit fires as signs of hope for the coming spring and the renewed power of the sun. Christians kept these popular traditions alive, and by the sixteenth century Catholics and Protestants throughout Germany used these symbols to celebrate their Advent hope in Christ, the everlasting Light. And from Germany the use of the Advent wreath spread throughout the Christian world.

There are three elements to the Advent wreath, of course: the evergreen branches that signify continuous life and resurrection; the circular shape that reminds us of God's unending

1

love and purpose for humankind; and the candles that speak of the light of Christ entering the world.

Advent means 'to come', and the Latin word for 'advent' is also the root of the word 'adventure'. As we move towards Christmas, we actually feel that we are embarking on a great adventure, the journey from dark into light, pregnancy to birth, anticipation to realization. And as part of this, Advent also heralds a significant shift in the Christian calendar, as we move from ordinary time – all those Sundays after Pentecost – to an extraordinary time: a time to linger in the darkness and prepare for the arrival into the world of God's light.

Back in those hot and glorious days of August 2003, I remember bumping into Rachel week after week at church and thinking 'Oh my goodness, the girl is going to burst!' Here at St Luke's we watched several women get bigger and bigger during that year. And every time you saw them you wanted to bring it all to a conclusion, to bring the waiting to an end. But that's what it's all about – expecting . . . waiting, hoping, anticipating, longing to see the tiny little baby wriggling around inside – who's also waiting . . . waiting to be born. And in a way it's a microcosm of life itself: life moves through constant cycles of expectancy and birth, darkness and light, hope and realization, winter and summer.

Advent is a time of pregnant waiting. And just as future parents must embrace the waiting, making preparations for what is to come, so Advent teaches us that we can't have everything right here, right now; we must enter the cycle, embrace the mystery of life and wait in hope.

It's a funny thing, I know, that the Gospel reading on Advent Sunday should be all about apocalyptic visions of disasters: signs in the heavens, war and distress all around, and ecological turmoil. But there's a clear logic to it all. It's now widely believed that many of the cataclysmic events Jesus prophesied in this chapter relate to the destruction of Jerusalem in AD 70 – at least ten years prior to Luke's writing of his Gospel, which is why he could write about it in such detail.

The believers to whom Luke addressed his writing had witnessed the terrors of Nero and the tumult that surrounded his downfall, and they were no doubt living in fear of their lives. Luke's recording of the prophecy Jesus gave is a way of reminding these early Christians that the ultimate fate of the world lies within the circle of God's eternal purpose and not in the hands of a vicious dictator.

As we rehearse the story of Christmas yet again this year, we will be reminded that this is exactly what the story teaches us: that despite the vicious efforts of a cruel despot, the circle of God's love could not be broken. And it's not just Christmas – the same message of God's unbroken love and purpose for creation is etched into the events of Easter, as it is in the very fabric of human history.

But how does the circle of divine love appear in our world? Where can we see it in an age of terrorist atrocities, pointless bloodshed, racial hatred and religious bigotry? The kingdom of God does not appear in political or military force; it's not about 'big is best' or 'might is right'. Rather, it is revealed in the power of vulnerability, the unstoppable strength of grace: 'Grace makes beauty out of ugly things', as a certain Irish band proclaims.

In his book *The Pilgrim Road*, Brian Gerrish gives a wonderful insight into how the circle of God's love enters our world:

> We look out on a scene of appalling hatred, bigotry, and violence, and we are tempted to despair of the human race. Then a face appears in the crowd to remind us of justice and mercy. The pattern of events is refigured. It becomes a story of human courage and decency, which lays a task on us, enlists our support, demands that we take sides. The mysterious force that moves our lives takes on a face, and

we are persuaded that justice and mercy too, like grace, are written into the constitution of our world. We see God's face, and we are saved. Saved from what? From the cynicism and despair, the resignation and indifference, that might otherwise turn us to stone.

The temptation of many Christians in the face of a world of despair is to turn away and look for some divine intervention from outside of the world; to look for an escape route in the second coming. Without wishing to detract from the prospect of Christ's appearing in this way, I would suggest that this is not where our attention should be focused.

As Karl Rahner, the great Catholic theologian, suggests, the second coming is perhaps better thought of as the world finally coming to Christ rather than as Christ returning to the world. The second coming shouldn't be thought of as the return of someone who has been absent, but as the breaking through to the whole world of a presence which has been continuous throughout history. And how does this presence of God appear? Through the face of God that Brian Gerrish identifies: the face of courage, love and mercy in the midst of despair.

When children are baptized we symbolically draw them and their families into the circle of God's love. It's not difficult with those we already know and love, is it? In these people we do indeed see the face of God. The real challenge is to lift our eyes beyond, to discern the face of God in unfamiliar features, perhaps threatening features – and draw the circle around them too. The challenge begins right here in our church, as we see new faces appearing week by week. St Luke's advertises itself as an inclusive church – may we live up to our own publicity; may we be a community that constantly draws its circles larger and larger, always including, never excluding.

Remember, the one whose birth we wait to celebrate

appeared in the world as a stranger: God incognito, hiding in a barn, appearing in unexpected places, hanging out with surprising people.

This is Advent: a time to slow down, explore the mystery, walk in the darkness of expectancy, set foot in the world of God's possibility. And, most of all, enter the ever-widening circle of divine love yet again.

Crib, cross and altar

Luke 2.1–7

Warnie Lewis came back from a bus trip to tell his brother Jack (C. S. Lewis) about a humorous event on his way home. As the bus rode by a church all decorated for Christmas, a woman pointed out of the window and exclaimed loudly, 'Just look at that, the church is taking over everything else and now they are trying to take over Christmas.'

Perhaps the most surprising thing about this story is that it dates back to the 1950s. Nowadays, when local councils, school governors and charity shops seem determined to squeeze out of Christmas any specific Christian content, we might understand someone imagining that 'the church is trying to take over Christmas', but clearly, the problem goes back a lot further.

And it's true: year on year the connection between the seasonal razzmatazz and the original meaning of Christmas is becoming more and more tenuous. Yet, despite lovely carols being done to death, despite people spending money they can't afford on presents that are neither needed nor wanted, despite plastic trees, red-nosed reindeers, gallons of booze and bellies filled to bursting point, I can't help thinking with Frederick Buechner that, for all our efforts, we've never quite managed to ruin Christmas.

There are probably many reasons for this. For a brief moment or two, the darkness of disenchantment, cynicism and doubt gives way to the mystery of a baby; a dream of innocence, the possibility of hope – and not even canned carols piped out in every shopping mall in the land from mid-November onwards can drown that out entirely.

Christmas is also the most universal of the Christian festivals. It's the feast of the incarnation, the great mystery of the word becoming flesh – God taking human form. The implication is that God in Christ does not just come for church-goers, for those who respond to the gospel message or for those who partake of the blessed sacraments. Every human being who has ever walked this planet shares the humanity God inhabits, and every human being is potentially healed by his taking their nature. Peace on earth and goodwill from God are not simply for the members of the God Squad, but for all peoples, for all time.

The truth is: the manger that became his crib, the birth of the Christ-child, is still among us, in our world, in our ordinary everyday world – yet so often we fail to see it.

Let me tell you a story about a young clergyman. He and his wife do all the usual things on Christmas Eve. They string the lights and hang the ornaments. They supervise the hanging of the stockings. They tuck the children in bed. They lug the presents down out of hiding and pile them under the tree. Just as they are about to fall into bed exhausted, the man remembers his neighbour's sheep. His is a rural parish and he has promised to feed the sheep while his neighbour is away, and with everything else going on, he has forgotten all about it.

So down the hill he goes, through knee-deep snow. He gets two bales of hay from the barn and carries them into the shed. There's a 40-watt bulb hanging by its cord from the low roof, and he switches it on. The sheep huddle in a corner, watching as he cuts the baling twine, shakes the squares of hay apart and starts scattering it. Then they come bumbling and shoving to get at it with their foolish, mild faces, the puffs of their breath showing in the air. He is reaching to turn off the light and leave when suddenly he realizes where he is. The winter darkness. The glimmer of light. The smell of hay and the sound of the animals eating. He's there. He's in the cattle shed with the manger.

He only just saw it. The man whose business it is to have an eye for such things is all but blind to what is there before him. The one who on his best days believes that everything that is most precious anywhere comes from that manger almost went home to bed without realizing that he had been in its presence. And we're all the same: even those of us who spend our entire lives embroiled in church business can so easily overlook the glorious truth that the whole world, the ordinary world, is the manger-crib. The Christ-child is being born again and again all around us, yet so often we fail to recognize him.

> And is it true? And is it true,
> This most tremendous tale of all,
> Seen in a stained-glass window's hue,
> A Baby in an ox's stall?
>
> John Betjeman

But is it not also true that in some wonderful sense this babe is born in every ox's stall, every maternity ward, every lover's kiss, every act of kindness in the face of hatred and injustice, every smile between friends, every loaf of bread or glass of wine shared, every gloriously ordinary, wonder-ful scrap of true life in this world? 'How silently, how silently, the won-drous gift is given!'

But perhaps the very strength of the Christmas story – the heavenly choir singing to poor shepherds in the fields, the young virgin mother, the innocence of a child – is also its weakness. It lends itself to sentimentality and unrealistic expectations. Remember the carol: the holly not only bears a white blossom of innocence, it also bears a berry 'as red as any blood'. Theologically speaking, the crib and the cross are both made from the same wood.

It's instructive to ponder that Mary was a part of both scenes: the crib and the cross. At the crib she teaches us the joy and wonder of saying 'yes' to God. At the cross she shows us how to stand in silent strength in the face of injustice, bereavement and pain. The crib symbolizes the unconditional gift of divine love; the cross manifests the extent to which that love will reach in encompassing all human sin and devastation.

To celebrate the mystery of Christ's birth without also embracing the mystery of his death inevitably leads to sentiment rather than true love. We cannot speak of Jesus' birth without reference to his death, any more than we can speak of his suffering death without acknowledging the wonder of Bethlehem.

But there's one further connection to make. In the crib we encounter the mystery of God incarnate in human flesh and blood; on the cross we find the mystery of God experiencing death in order that we may know the depth of the divine embrace. But it is in ordinary bread and wine consecrated on the altar that the mystery of God's real presence with us today is known and experienced week in, week out. The wonder of the Eucharist is that it is here in bread and wine that we realize the incarnation afresh, the reality that God hangs out with flawed human beings, that he inhabits a damaged world, sharing in its pain and suffering, and offering paths of wholeness and healing.

Theologically speaking, the crib, the cross and the altar are all made from one wood.

> And is it true? For if it is,
> No loving fingers tying strings
> Around those tissued fripperies,

The sweet and silly Christmas things,
Bath salts and inexpensive scent
And hideous tie so kindly meant,

No love that in a family dwells,
No carolling in frosty air,
Nor all the steeple-shaking bells
Can with this single Truth compare –
That God was Man in Palestine
And lives today in Bread and Wine.

John Betjeman

Let us celebrate the Great Nativity by eating and drinking afresh of the holy mysteries through which the boundless love of the crucified Christ is showered upon us.

Star-gazers

Isaiah 60.1–6; Matthew 2.1–12

My wife Pat and I rent a rather primitive cottage in North Yorkshire, called High Coalsgarth. It's about two miles from the nearest road (access up a tiny track through five gates), it has no electricity, a dodgy water supply and a chemical toilet. But it stands on the side of a hill, with fantastic views of the little valley that we share with lapwings, curlews, a pair of buzzards and a heron that fishes in the brook that runs down past the house.

There are so many things we love about High Coalsgarth, and it doesn't much matter to us about the time of year or the weather – we love it all. But one of the things we adore most of all is the crisp clear winter nights – and the sky. Without artificial light anywhere around, the sense of the heavens above is overwhelming. My favourite thing is to lie on the hard frosty ground and gaze at the teeming millions of stars, and the dazzling splendour of the Milky Way where all the stars just merge together in a misty haze.

Something fascinates us about the stars, doesn't it? Believe it or not, my own fascination with the night sky started in Liverpool – where you haven't the remotest chance of discerning the Milky Way. I swapped my bike with a kid at school for his telescope. My dad wasn't too impressed with the deal, but I was 'over the moon'! I ended up spending hours lying on the roof of our back shed, peering at craters on the moon and trying to identify Mars and Jupiter. I remember writing to the Royal Astronomical Society in London – which seemed as far away as the nearest star – for maps of the moon and the night sky.

But we're all star-gazers. We're all fascinated by the heavens. Remember Hale-Bopp, the comet that sailed through our skies back in 1998? We had a fantastic view of it from the cottage on our Easter break that year. But all across the land thousands gathered at every imaginable vantage point to get a once-in-a-lifetime experience. Some had binoculars or telescopes, but the vast majority just stood and gazed – at a spot of light with a long tail out there in the darkness. The cynics reminded us that it was only a block of ice and rock. But for most people it was much more. It was an experience – maybe even a transcendent experience – a sign, perhaps, of the vastness of space beyond the comet, the outer reaches of the universe, or the great mystery of Being itself.

The word 'epiphany' means a 'manifestation' or 'appearing'. Apart from its specific religious meaning, it's used to describe a flash of revelation or realization, a moment of 'eureka'. And the short season of Epiphany in the church calendar is there to make the point that Christianity is a eureka kind of faith: it revolves around the belief that God chooses to be revealed to human beings, and that this revelation is the basis upon which new realities can be imagined. The story of the epiphany of the magi highlights the fact that divine revelation can appear in many different ways – in this instance, through pagan astrology!

Of course, we have no way of knowing whether the story of the magi is true. But what matters much more to me is that the early Christians chose to include this story in the Gospel narrative, and that human longing for a new reality was linked to gazing at stars.

I recently got around to watching a film I've wanted to see for ages: *Amistad*. It's based on the true story of 20 or 30

Africans who were ambushed in Sierra Leone and sold into slavery, and shipped to the West Indies aboard a Spanish boat called *La Amistad*. On the high seas, the slaves rebelled against their captors and took over the ship. Eventually they were captured by American sailors and handed over to the authorities. And the main story of the film follows a series of fascinating trials in Washington, the outcome of which probably contributed to the start of the Civil War.

In the opening scenes of the film, Cinque, one of the Africans, whose people have just taken over the ship and are attempting to sail back to their homeland in Africa, gazes up into the teeming starlit sky above the boat. He wonders about the vastness of the universe and the manifestation of this heavenly light to a mostly hostile world. But it isn't just for inspiration, as he looks at the sky. Cinque recognizes the familiar patterns, and he wants to be guided by them in his search for home.

The film is about epiphany, how the light comes to illumine the dimness of human minds, and how difficult the human struggle for freedom, grace and enlightenment can be. But it's also about guiding principles – the search for self-evident truths and inalienable rights.

Star-gazing can be a spiritual experience. I guess it's to do with perspective. When we want to see new possibilities, we say 'the sky's the limit'. In other words: there are no limits. An open sky reminds us that limits are self-imposed: there are always other possibilities, other realities. And that's why star-gazing needn't simply mean passive observation; it also becomes the basis for action and for change.

As each new year begins to unfold, we must follow the magi and become star-gazers instead of navel-gazers. Navel-gazers can't see beyond themselves – their own selfish desires, their own creature comforts, their own self-imposed horizons of vision. Star-gazers forget about themselves, as they become part of a bigger picture. They dare to believe that something else is possible, that change can happen, that the way things have been need not determine the way things might be.

The magi weren't *just* star-gazers, they were also adventurers. Their vision was not limited to what they already knew. Here were people who were prepared to leave their familiar surroundings, prepared to explore beyond their box, prepared to recognize God in other forms. How fantastic that the early Christians could incorporate such a generous story in their account of Christ's birth, a story of people journeying to God, not through scripture, or the voice of the prophets, or church tradition, but through the guidance of the stars interpreted with pagan wisdom.

I believe that people are by nature star-gazers, that a longing for God exists in every human heart. It's what T. S. Eliot called 'the still point of the turning world'. Or what St Augustine meant when he said: 'You have made us for yourself, and our hearts are restless until they rest in you.' The church's task is to connect with this God-longing in people, however it is expressed, or whatever form it takes. And, personally, I find it doesn't take too long to encounter the God-longing in most people.

But sadly, instead of making these connections, all too often the church is caught up with its own navel-gazing issues – more concerned with an agenda for its own survival than with the agenda of God's kingdom in the world. Bear in mind that in the beginning the church was a by-product of the kingdom of God, not the other way around. All too frequently I see the church dismissing the gifts of the magi in today's world – busily excluding those people whom God is *in*cluding.

Maybe it's to do with power: in the wider world it's the norm for politics to be dominated by navel-gazing attitudes and policies. As we contemplate the intransigence of so many situations around the world, we're left wondering when leaders of imagination will emerge who will forget their own belly-button politics and set their eyes on the guiding star.

The reason we constantly come back to Nelson Mandela as an example of such leadership is that there are so few people like him. Perhaps 27 years' imprisonment taught him to gaze at the stars.

Each new year we listen again to the story that has been retold thousands of times over the past two millennia. It's significant that the Epiphany story of star-gazing, journey and adventure, of barriers broken and borders traversed, should fall at the beginning of the year, a time when we naturally review our priorities, revisiting unmet goals and shattered dreams.

We need to refocus our vision, to get our eye back on the star. And where will it stop in today's world? Where is our Bethlehem?

'With whom I am well pleased'

Genesis 1.1–5; Mark 1.4–11

There's a great story about Albert Einstein, when he was at Princeton in New Jersey. It's said that as he walked in front of a local inn on his way to work one day, he was mistaken for a bellboy by a wealthy middle-aged woman who had just arrived in a luxury sedan. She ordered him to carry her luggage into the hotel. Einstein did exactly as he was bidden, received a small tip, and then continued to his office to ponder the mysteries of the universe. True or not, this story conjures up a delightful image – the ruffled figure of this little man, the most celebrated intellect of our time, doffing his cap as he is given a 50-cent piece.

It's interesting that Mark's Gospel has no Christmas story at all. The narrative begins with the baptism of Jesus at the River Jordan – an event that, unlike Christmas, appears in all four Gospels. This was the public unveiling of Jesus – his Epiphany – before which lie 30 years of anonymity. The people who saw Jesus growing up, or who breezed in and out of Joseph's workshop to purchase a new chair or get their plough repaired, hadn't the faintest clue as to his divine identity. This guy to whom they probably slipped the odd denarius did not only ponder the mysteries of the universe – he created them.

But there are so many questions to be asked. How much did Mary tell Jesus about the strange circumstances surrounding his birth – angelic visitations, shepherds appearing out of nowhere, weird travellers from the east bearing mysterious gifts? And whatever happened to the gifts? Did Joseph ever broach the subject of his hasty marriage to Mary? And at what point in those 30 silent years did Jesus cotton on to his identity? How about his cousin John: when did he come to the conclusion that he wasn't worthy to untie the thong on the sandals of his childhood pal Jesus? I certainly have no idea.

But just imagine what a spectacular event this baptism at Jordan was. I have seen a few interesting baptisms in my time. I recall my first ever river baptism – in North Yorkshire. I was very nervous because I had an 18-stone woman to dunk, and with a strong current in the Ure I had visions of her floating dowstream. At the time I was assisted by the equivalent of a curate, so I marched him down to the river earlier in the week to have a practice. Thankfully I managed to deliver Mrs Bell safely to the riverbank after her dipping.

But this baptism of Jesus was like no other before or since. As John pulled his cousin out of the water, the heavens were torn open, and as the Spirit descended upon Jesus in the form of a dove, a thunderous voice declared, 'You are my Son, the Beloved; with you I am well pleased.'

It's a funny thing, isn't it – God being pleased? I mean, the whole notion of what the Almighty feels is surely way beyond our comprehension. There's an old Yiddish saying that 'When people talk about God, God laughs.' Even the name of the Hebrew God was deliberately unpronounceable as a way of acknowledging his total otherness. But hey, watch out – he speaks! (probably in English with a Jewish accent) and says, 'This is my Son. I'm pleased with him.'

This is a profound theological statement. God, the God we worship today, is a God who feels pleasure. I have to say that my own church upbringing left me with the distinct impression that God did displeasure much better than he did pleasure! But that's not the picture we have in our Gospel story.

The Bible passages in Genesis and Mark are both about beginnings: one about the beginning of Jesus' public ministry, the other about the beginning of everything. And the two correspond in significant ways. For example, the Spirit appears in both narratives: in Genesis as a great wind sweeping across the face of the primordial deep, and in the Gospel as a dove descending on the River Jordan.

Also, in both accounts God speaks, and on both occasions God is pleased. In Genesis, we're told that he beheld the fruit of each day's work and declared it good, which presumably meant he was pleased or satisfied with what he saw. In a book called *The Human Adventure*, William McNamara puts it like this: 'On each successive day of creation, from the beginning to the end, God looks at it and says: "Good! Very Good! Terrific! Wonderful!" He looks at the way the grapes grow in California, the way they become wine and make people merry; and he says: "Yes, that's it; do it again!"'

So God is a being who experiences pleasure. And God isn't only pleased with the glories of creation, or with his Son, Jesus Christ – God is pleased with you and me. That's not to say he is pleased with everything we say or do; we all know that cannot be true. Sin is in some way intrinsic to our humanity. But as Christians we proclaim a crucified God who chooses to counter human sin and evil in the ultimate demonstration of love and self-sacrifice. God is in the business of redemption, and he redeems everything and everyone who will be redeemed. And so, in baptism we are declared to be children of God, accepted in the beloved, subjects of divine pleasure.

Yet, even though at times we fail to live up to our own best expectations of ourselves, let alone God's, we are also made in the divine image. And every time we behave or respond in a manner that reflects that image – through relationships, or creativity, or work, or play, or in simple acts of kindness – God again pronounces us 'very good'. And how do we know this? How can we know that God is pleased with us? *We know God is pleased when we feel God's pleasure within us.*

The classic 1980s film *Chariots of Fire* is the story of Eric Liddell, a Scottish athlete who ran for Great Britain in the Olympics after the First World War. Eric's parents were missionaries in China, where he had grown up. And both he and his sister Jenny were deeply religious people.

Almost as soon as Eric receives his invitation to run in the Olympics, a message arrives from his parents asking him to go immediately to help them in their work in China. So far as Jenny is concerned, there is no competition: Eric must follow the call of God to serve as a missionary. He must choose to work for God's glory rather than run for his own.

It is a painful decision for Eric. He cares for his parents and plans to work as a missionary after the Olympics. He trys to explain to his sister the importance of his running: 'Jenny, Jenny, God made me fast, and when I run I feel God's pleasure.'

And he did run, in his own idiosyncratic way – arms flailing, head back, mouth open, hair blowing in the wind. He ran as a wild animal runs, unselfconsciously, wholeheartedly, nothing held back. 'When I run, I feel God's pleasure.'

It doesn't matter what we do in life, there's something very important about wholeheartedness, giving ourselves to whatever it is we have to do, nothing held back – then we feel God's pleasure. And when we know the pleasure of God, doors and windows fly open and chains of past wounds are released. We find ourselves filled with the wind of the Holy Spirit – a rushing wind drives us forward, arms flailing, head back, mouth open, wind in our hair.

As Jesus stood waist deep in the River Jordan, his heart

was wide open to God. Did he know what lay ahead? Had he any real idea why he was submitting himself to baptism? But it was through doing this that the windows of heaven were thrown open, and he heard the astounding words: 'You are my child, my beloved.' Yet I'm sure that despite the uniqueness of the occasion the pleasure of God was no new experience for Jesus. He had sensed the delight of God repeatedly, on his mother's lap, in the joys of childhood, in the 'Well done!' of Joseph as a young carpenter's apprentice, in the satisfaction of pushing the sharp blade of a plane along a sweet-smelling piece of timber, in the warm glow of a glass of red wine with friends on a Mediterranean evening. The sense of divine pleasure was nothing strange to Jesus of Nazareth.

And I am certain that each one of us has felt the pleasure of God. It would be pretty difficult to get through childhood without experiencing God's pleasure. Children are infections of divine pleasure. A friend of mine tells of how as a young boy he used to ride around the Sussex lanes on his bike. Wind in his hair, breathing in the warm summer air, he would sing in gobbledegook at the top of his voice. That, for me, is the true essence of speaking (singing) in tongues – bathing in the pleasure of God.

Churches should be places where we experience God's delight. Sadly, far too many people leave church feeling worse than when they arrived. The Westminster Shorter Catechism affirms that humanity's chief end is 'to worship God, and to enjoy him for ever'. That's not to say that we only sense God's pleasure in religious activities (it would probably be in short supply if that were the case); rather, it means that any activity in which we experience divine pleasure *is* potentially worship – regardless of whether or not we know about or believe the Christian message.

I believe it is God's pleasure, God's delight in the goodness of the world, that lies at the very core of all true human pleasure. In doing those things that are truly a fulfilment of our human potential, we are much closer to God than we imagine, or even care to believe.

To experience the pleasure of another person, let alone God, is a wondrous privilege. It's tempting simply to bathe in such attention. And yet to do so is to sink into the dark crevice of self-indulgence. Love must be reciprocal. Jesus did not linger at Jordan, grasping a sacred moment; rather, he carried the divine pleasure with him as he went forth, first through the painful choices of the wilderness, and then into a life of caring for others. God does not call us simply to be on the receiving end of creation; we are also called to be co-creators with God. Energized by divine pleasure, we share in the divine impulse to create in love.

Some lovely words from the Christian writer and mystic Madeleine L'Engle express this far better than I can:

In that first epiphany, when matter was formless and space was empty, God created. How marvellous that there should be something rather than nothing! How marvellous that there is rather than there is not.

God created, and it was joy: time, space, matter. There is and we are part of that is-ness, part of that becoming. That is our calling: co-creation. Every single one of us without exception, is called to create with God. No one is too unimportant to have a share in the making or unmaking of the final showing-forth. Everything we do either draws the kingdom of love closer, or pushes it further off. That is a fearful responsibility, but when God made 'man in his own image', male and female responsibility went with it. Too often we let somebody else do it, the preacher, or the teacher, or the government agency. But if we are to continue to grow in God's image, then we have to accept responsibility.

We are beloved of God. We are the subject of divine pleasure. Let us go out into the world to bring the kingdom of love and peace into being.

Conversations with God

---

1 Samuel 3.1–20; John 1.43–51

What an amazing thing a TV remote is. What an incredible aid to parenthood – provided you keep a firm grasp on it, rather than letting your kids get hold of it. You can just flip the channel as soon as you realize something is appearing that you don't want the little critters to see. Actually, it also works equally well when older relatives are visiting. I well recall those occasions when my finger wasn't quite fast enough when my mother-in-law was with us. How I loved those sermonettes about 'filth and vulgarity on the television'.

Yes, I like the remote. And nowadays you can just flip away through 30-odd channels if you've got cable or a dish. What amazes me about that is the thought of all those TV and radio programmes swishing around in the atmosphere. Films, game shows, 24-hour news, current affairs, sitcoms, evangelical preachers ranting on, heated debates – it's all out there all of the time. All around us now there's an almighty cacophony raging away. Images, words, messages – they're everywhere, all around us. But you can't hear or see them unless you're tuned in with a radio or TV.

The Bible passage about Samuel is a great one, isn't it? Many of us grew up on stories like this in Sunday school. But what a funny old thing to say: 'The word of God was rare in those days.' What does that mean? Was the Almighty going through a quiet patch? Had he run out of ideas of what to say? Or was he sulking, because people didn't take much notice when he did speak?

Much as I'd like to speculate, perhaps we should ask who was making the observation in the first place. We don't really know who the narrator was: the book is drawn from several different sources. But we do know that it's a human observation. And I guess what it really means is that there were few prophets around at this point in Israel's history. And of course this is the story of the calling of one of the greatest prophets the Hebrew people ever witnessed: Samuel.

But saying that there were few prophets around is quite different from saying that God had given up speaking. It's my view that God is always speaking, everywhere in his world. Rather like radio and TV, the airwaves are literally packed with messages from the divine – but you've got to tune in to pick them up.

It's not always easy to interpret a story like the one about Samuel. Did he really hear an audible voice? Does God speak like that to people today? Well, I've never heard the audible voice of God myself. That said, there are people who testify to hearing God speak in that way. Some years ago, when I was a handsome young man, in the church I went to there were two young women who each believed God had spoken to them and told them to marry me. As it goes, he hadn't mentioned the matter to me. And it would have taken more than an audible voice to get me to the altar with either of them – it would probably have needed a battalion of angels as well!

Having said that, I wouldn't wish to discount the possibility of people hearing God speak in an audible voice. But we need to bear in mind that there are only two such instances recorded in the life of Jesus, and on one of those he says the voice was for the sake of others who heard it and not for him. All in all, I think if God spoke to me in an audible voice,

I'd feel it was a sign that I wasn't very good at listening to God's voice, generally.

The story of Samuel and Eli is salutary. Here's Eli, the epitomy of the institutional priesthood, completely tuned out to God's voice. He allowed his bullying, depraved sons, Hophni and Phinehas, to operate in the priestly office, bringing shame on themselves and their family. God was speaking to both Samuel and Eli that night, but only Samuel was tuned in. And what a message it was that Samuel heard: 'See, I am about to do something in Israel that will make both ears of anyone who hears of it tingle.' No wonder Eli was tuned out. Sometimes the message can be hard. We don't *want* to hear.

But on a personal point, I would have to say that it has been the most painful things God has said to me that have proven, in the long run, to be the most powerful and helpful in getting me on track.

Nathanael (the man who Philip brought to Jesus in the Gospel reading) was much more like Samuel than Eli. Jesus described him as an 'Israelite in whom there is no deceit'. What a fantastic thing to say about someone – no deceit. And do you know what's great about this? When Philip invited his friend to come and meet Jesus, Nathanael had responded with a bit of local banter (there was rivalry between the people of Cana and those from Nazareth). 'Can any good thing come out of Nazareth?', he says. I'll go with Jesus' judgement: this was a man with a sense of humour, not a tribal bigot.

But most important of all, Nathanael is someone with an openness of spirit. Some may see his ready response to Jesus as naïve, even gullible. I don't think so. Of course, I'm just guessing; we know very little about this man. But I do know Nathanael-like people: people with an enviable ability to rise above cynicism, even in the face of repeated disappointments. The image of Nathanael sitting under the fig tree is quite revealing. Symbolic of peace and security, the shelter of the fig tree was a common place for reflective thought and meditation – perhaps a good spot for 'tuning in'.

This is what I find so helpful about saying daily prayers. It offers the space and time to deliberately tune in to God. The opening lines of Morning Prayer from *Common Worship* never cease to turn me Godwards:

The night has passed, and the day lies open before us;
let us pray with one heart and mind.

We silently contemplate the day ahead, then continue:

As we rejoice in the gift of this new day,
so may the light of your presence, O God,
set our hearts on fire with love for you;
now and for ever . . .

It is so important to acknowledge each new day as a gift; to recognize that it lies open before us, like a sheet of paper waiting to be written on, or a canvas inviting paint. Most of us can find a few minutes somewhere in the day to be quiet, to reflect, to be open to God and to our own inner thoughts and feelings. Some people find it helpful to have a simple structure to work with, as at morning prayers.

Prayer and meditation are ways of listening. But how does God speak? The only voices I actually hear at morning prayers are those of people present, yet God does speak to me. Often I'm reminded of things I must do, people I must see; things I otherwise tend to push to the back of my mind are brought forward. Sometimes I experience what I think are God's feelings about situations or people. Or I see things about myself in clearer focus. Creative silence is a very necessary part of prayer. Pascal once commented that 'most of man's troubles come from his not being able to sit quietly in his chamber'. And I have to say that my personal spiritual

life would be greatly impoverished were it not for very atten-
tive times of sitting on the loo.

So prayer is (or should be) a form of listening. But the
reverse is also true: listening, observing and doing things can
also be forms of prayer. As I said, God is a speaking God: the
world is a tumult of divine messages, if only we will tune in
to hear them. Helmut Thielicke, the German theologian,
expresses the same thought in a slightly different way:

> At the beginning of the war I stood in the bell tower of St
> Katherine's Church in Danzig with the church organist. He
> sat at the keyboard of the carillon to play a hymn on the
> hour. His mighty proclamation of the gospel rang out over
> the whole town. The bells beat upon my ears and the
> sound of their message so filled me that no other sound
> could intervene. Far below, though, I could see people
> going on about their business. They were building an air-
> raid shelter. The excavator clattered, pneumatic drills
> hammered away, and traffic surged along. No one looked
> up to listen to the music that was pounding in my ears and
> filling me to the brim. What sounded all around us up
> above remained inaudible down there below amidst the
> noise of daily work.
>
> Have we heard the sound that comes from above? We
> certainly cannot stop our machines. Nor should we try. But
> we can pay attention to the sound that filters through our
> earthly noise. For the air is full of promises, and we would
> lose everything if we failed to hear them.

God speaks to me on the loo. Lots of people find that God
says things to them while they are travelling, or walking the
dog, or hoovering. Some people find it helpful to write things
down; some (like me) hear God when they are talking to
other people. We're all different.

And what about the middle of the night? That's when God

called to Samuel. Sadly, when I'm awake in the middle of the night I tend to be listening to my anxieties. So the challenge I face is to learn to tune out from fears and worries in the sleepless hours of the night, and to tune in to the reassuring voice of God. And God is always 'on air'; messages of hope and vivacity are constantly being broadcast – even in the darkness of your bedroom, or in those messy, difficult bits of life when you feel desperate and all alone. It's just a case of 'turning on and tuning in', as we used to say in the 1960s.

But beware: your life may never be the same again. Nathanael was destined for an exciting, turbulent, life of laughter, adventure and tears, following the most incredible man he'd ever met – ultimately to a dark and bloody hill called Golgotha.

This short excerpt from Anne Tyler's book *The Clock Winder* epitomizes both the ordinariness and the transforming potential in listening to God.

I'll tell you how I happened to start working at the school. I was leaning out the window of this crafts shop where I used to sell things, watching a parade go by. There were people crammed on both sidewalks, mothers with babies and little children, fathers with children on their shoulders. And suddenly I was so surprised by them. Isn't it amazing how hard people work to raise their children? Human beings are born so helpless, and stay helpless so long. For every grown-up you see, you know there must be at least one person who had the patience to lug them around, and feed them, and walk them nights and keep them out of danger for years and years without a break. Teaching them how to fit into civilization and how to talk back and forth with other people, taking them to zoos and parades and educational events, telling them all those nursery rhymes and word-of-mouth fairy tales. Isn't that surprising? People you wouldn't trust your purse with five minutes, maybe, but still they put in years and years of time tending their children along and they don't even make a fuss about it. Even if it's a criminal they turn out, or some other kind of failure – still, he managed to get grown, didn't he? Isn't that something? . . .

Well, there I was hanging out the window . . . thinking all this over. Then I thought, What am I doing here, anyway? Up in this shop where I'm bored stiff? And never moving on to something else, for fear of some harm I might cause? You'd think I was some kind of special case, I thought, but I'm not! I'm like all the people I'm sitting here gawking at, and I might just as well stumble on out and join them! So right that day I quit my job, and started casting about for new work. And found it – teaching crafts in a reform school. Well, you might not think the girls there would be all that great, but I like them. Wasn't that something? Just from one little old parade.

Be careful, little ears, what you hear!

Thin places

———•◦•———

2 Corinthians 3.12—4:2; Luke 9.28–36

One of the great benefits in having a dog is that you get some regular exercise. Most days my wife Pat and I try to take Woody for a run on Hampstead Heath. Usually we end up wandering around Parliament Hill. There are two things I love about this. First, being on Hampstead Heath can, depending on which way you look, give the illusion that you are actually in the country. But the other thing is that if you look the other way you can see the whole of London. And it's amazing what a different perspective on the city you get from up there.

It's great to pick out the Clock Tower on North Road. From there it's not difficult to shift your focus and spot the steeple of St Luke's. The whole of the parish is contracted to about ten inches. I always like to mutter a prayer or two for the 12,336 souls who inhabit our little patch of North London.

It's amazing how short a distance you have to climb in order to get a completely new perspective on things. While our church tower was surrounded by scaffolding recently, I used to clamber up the 155 feet for a bird's-eye view. It's funny, but there's something about high places that makes you want to pray – well, they have that effect on me, anyway. While I was up there I did two things: I took some photographs of the parish, and I prayed for the people of St Luke's, West Holloway. Actually, the photos are *visual* prayers.

The mountain that Jesus climbed with his three friends, Peter, James and John, required a little more effort than a stroll up Parliament Hill. Mount Tabor, where it's thought the transfiguration took place, rises 1,900 feet above the Plain of Esdraelon. Nazareth lies six miles to the west, and the steep ascent offers magnificent views of the whole area.

But the vision revealed to the disciples that day was one no other visitor to the Tabor peak had ever had the privilege of viewing. They had gone to the mountain to pray, but understandably they were distracted by tiredness from the climb. Then they witnessed a sight that made them rub their eyes in disbelief: while praying, Jesus was transformed before them. His face changed and his clothes became dazzling white. And the two figures of Moses and Elijah were there, large as life, talking with Jesus about what was going to happen when he arrived at Jerusalem.

It's a strange and mysterious account. New Testament scholars struggle to know what to make of it. The more sceptical argue that the transfiguration has no basis in fact: the story is a metaphor, a visual assertion of the early church's faith that Jesus was indeed the Messiah. Others suggest that Luke was describing a post-resurrection encounter with the risen Jesus experienced by some of the disciples. I'm more inclined to the idea of John Macquarrie, that throughout the ministry of Jesus there *were* pointers forward to the climax which came only at the end. What Macquarrie calls 'gleams of glory' gave a continuity between Jesus' life and ministry and his resurrection.

But it's interesting that the humanness of Jesus was never obliterated by visions of his glory. I like the way Frederick Buechner puts it in his book *Whistling in the Dark*:

It was Jesus of Nazareth all right, the man they had tramped many a dusty mile with, whose mother and brothers they knew, the one they'd seen as hungry, tired, footsore as the rest of them. But it was also the Messiah, the Christ, in his glory. It was the holiness of the man shining through his humanness, his face so afire with it that they were almost blinded.

But it's a mistake to see the transfiguration simply as something to do with Jesus. It's also about us: we also are called to holiness or inner wholeness. Now this is nothing to do with being pious or 'holier than thou'; it's to do with integrity, with inner calm and connectedness. St Paul says that we too can be transformed (transfigured: it's the same word) from one degree of glory to another.

And how does this transfiguring happen? Paul says that it happens as we see the glory of the Lord. Now that can sound a bit other-worldly, but I assure you it isn't. Basically, we are transformed when we learn to recognize those 'gleams of glory'. We all have them – tiny gleams, maybe, but gleams of glory all the same.

Gleams of glory are all around us: an undeserved smile from a little child, the faces of parents playing with their children on a roundabout in the park, an eyeful of the Milky Way on a moonless night far away from the city, a pint of cool beer on a summer's day, standing barefoot in the sand, the sight of the city cleansed by a recent fall of snow. And we all know about that look of sheer excitement that momentarily transfigures the human face so that great rays of glory shine through.

If we're lucky we find places where we can almost be assured of finding some gleams of glory. In the last chapter of A. A. Milne's *The House at Pooh Corner* there's an enchanted place where Christopher Robin says his final goodbye to Pooh. It's called Galleons Lap. 'Sitting there', we are told, 'they could see the whole world spread out until it reached the sky, and whatever there was all the world over was with them in Galleons Lap.'

The idea of places where heaven and earth meet is very ancient. Special large trees or mountains evoked in our ancestors feelings of transcendence – like Christopher Robin and Pooh, they felt that such a place was the central pivot of the earth or the entire cosmos. The technical word for such places is *axis mundi* – the hub of the world. Christians throughout the centuries have seen the cross as just this: an *axis mundi*, the heart of everything, the place where heaven and earth meet.

In a similar vein, in Celtic tradition there are places where the veil between the eternal and the temporal, the heavenly and the mundane, the spiritual and the material is very thin. It's almost as if you could put your hand through the divide. The island of Iona has always been such a place. George MacLeod, the late founder of the Iona Community, described Iona as 'a thin place where only tissue paper separates the material from the spiritual'.

What about you? Where are your thin places? Let me tell you about the funeral of Marie, who had been married to Harry for 60 years. Standing a few yards from the grave after the committal I watched with awe as Harry threw a single red rose on to his wife's coffin and then spoke to her for a whole minute, gesturing lovingly with his hands. I couldn't hear what he said. I didn't want to; the moment was too sacred. I was overwhelmed by the thinness of the tissue that separated Harry and Marie in that place. Just a year later I was privileged to lay Harry to rest in the same grave, sensing that the tissue was finally brushed aside. Gravesides can be thin places.

A thin place is anywhere where the visible and the invisible, the natural and the spiritual, the human and the divine become permeable. Some places seem to have that quality about them permanently. But sometimes totally ordinary, everyday places can suddenly become 'thin'. I love C. S. Lewis's idea of making a commonplace wardrobe into a gateway to Narnia; a mundane piece of furniture is transfigured into a mysterious passageway to a land beyond.

It may be a piece of music, a work of art, a moment of pause, a prayer, a smile from a stranger, a dank autumn afternoon in a Yorkshire dale, the song of a blackbird in Caledonian Park, an act of unexpected kindness ... almost anything can offer a gleam of glory, a stairway to heaven.

Actually, standing around the communion table can feel pretty thin at times. The sight of open palms waiting to receive the bread of life often sends a shudder of awe down my spine. The great web of relationships connected with this church past and present; traditions that stretch back centuries, re-enacted with a fresh glint in the eye; sacred stories, holy rituals drawing new generations into the cycle of life. Thin places, gleams of glory, shudders of excitement. Like the disciples in the story, we want it to last for ever. But Jesus leads us back down the mountain to the realities of life where a vision of glory can help us make the world a better place.

The wonder of thin places or gleams of glory is that we experience, in a moment, profound connectedness with all that matters – like Pooh and Christopher Robin, who felt that 'whatever there was all the world over was with them in Galleons Lap'. Let me end with some lovely words from Henri Nouwen:

At some moments we experience complete unity within us and around us. This may happen when we stand on a mountaintop and are captivated by the view. It may happen when we witness the birth of a child or the death of a friend. It may happen when we have an intimate conversation or a family meal. It may happen in church during a service or in a quiet room during prayer. But wherever and however it happens we say to ourselves: 'This is it ... everything fits ... all I ever hoped for is here. This is the experience that Peter, James and John had on the top of

Mount Tabor when they saw the aspect of Jesus' face change and his clothing become sparkling white. They wanted that moment to last forever. This is the experience of the fullness of time. These moments are given to us so that we can remember them when God seems far away and everything appears empty and useless. These experiences are true moments of grace.

Images of God

Psalm 27; Luke 13:31–35

While spending a few days up at our cottage in Yorkshire, Pat and I saw an amazing sight. One crisp but beautifully bright day, we were sitting on the bench outside the house with a cup of coffee, gazing across the valley. Then, about three or four yards in front of us, a little animal walked along the dry stone wall. It was a weasel – presumably a female because it was carrying a tiny, wriggling baby weasel in its mouth. After a few moments she ran back along the wall. And then, to our delight, she appeared again with another of her babies. Over a period of about 15 minutes we watched this wonderful little creature transport her entire litter, presumably to a safer nest site.

Watching the care, diligence and energy with which this whole exercise was carried out, I began to think about the words of Jesus from the Gospel of Luke: 'Jerusalem, Jerusalem . . . How often have I desired to gather your children together as a hen gathers her brood under her wings.'

Jesus is addressing himself to a city that has killed prophets and stoned messengers of God who were sent to it. Yet here he speaks, not with harsh judgement, but with moving compassion, drawing on warm maternal imagery to express the heart of God for his people. Little wonder that as we watched that little weasel mother ferrying her precious 'cargo' to safety we felt that something of the divine nature was being mirrored before us in the Yorkshire countryside.

That said, the Son of God likening himself to a hen is a bit weird. The Bible uses lots of creaturely metaphors to describe God, but no one ever dared to suggest a similarity to a chicken. Whatever happened to the mighty eagle or the majestic lion? But Jesus didn't even compare himself with a proud cockerel; he said he was like a mother hen.

The context adds to the strangeness of the imagery. Some Pharisees approached Jesus, saying something like: 'You'd better clear off, mate. King Herod is after you; and he's really on the warpath. If he catches you you're dead meat.' To which Jesus replies: 'Do me a favour, will you? Go and tell that fox to bog off!' A fox. Now that's interesting, because foxes eat chickens – and they're especially partial to a juicy little chick or two. And unless the hen has a sawn-off shot-gun tucked under its wing it really is dead meat.

And yet, in a way, there's absolutely no surprise here: Jesus had a habit of turning conventional wisdom on its head. He's the one who taught about greatness by holding up a child. He's the one who said that the meek rather than the ruthless and powerful would inherit the earth. He's the one who conquered evil by being executed between two criminals. Through his words and his actions Jesus taught us that true greatness is revealed in sacrifice for others, that real power is manifest in weakness.

Indeed, Jesus utterly redefined the meaning of success. He accumulated no worldly wealth – even his tomb was borrowed – he chose a bunch of no-hopers to change the entire history of the world, and the first witnesses to his resurrection were a couple of women, whose status in a patriarchal society was little more than that of beasts.

But at the heart of Jesus' new order was a totally reconfigured vision of God. The distant deity, shrouded in smoke, darkness, gloom and tempest, who handed down the law to Moses, is transformed into a loving father gazing from his window, longing for the return of his wayward son, or into a widow searching for a lost coin, or a mother hen longing to gather her wandering chicks under her wings.

And Jesus didn't transform our visions of God simply by introducing new doctrines or mental conceptions of God; he did it by giving an entirely new 'feel' to God. And 'feel' is very important to the way we humans perceive or respond to things. Advertisers understand this all too well. For example, when car manufacturers want us to buy a car, they don't try to impress us with technical specifications like compression ratio or maximum torque. No, they hit us with a TV commercial that sells us a whole feel about what it's like to own and drive this car – it will make you the strong, independent woman you really want to be; it will make you the coolest guy around and surround you with gorgeous women; it will transport you from daily drudgery to a land of dreams. It's all a load of rubbish, of course, but it makes the point that we don't really make decisions just on the basis of rational thinking.

So what kind of 'feel' do you have of God? Someone told me recently that they felt as though God was like an examiner marking his exam paper – and almost everything was being marked wrong. Others speak of God as a policeman, or a disapproving father. The interesting thing is that these descriptions come from deeply committed Christians who can recite all the right doctrines about a loving and forgiving God. But their inner pictures of God are in painful contradiction to their rational theories about him. And I can tell you that this sort of conflict is far from rare.

In his classic book *God of Surprises*, Gerard Hughes talks about Fred, who was considered a model Christian. Fred was married, he belonged to several voluntary bodies, took an intelligent interest in theology, lived a very simple lifestyle, rarely dined out or went to the theatre or the cinema, and spent most of his holidays with his wife at Christian conferences. At one such conference he attended a session led by Gerard Hughes, who encouraged him to pray using his imagination on scenes from the Gospels, picturing himself as a participant in the story. Fred related to Gerard his encounter with the marriage at Cana.

He pictured a sumptuous feast, with dancing, singing and great merriment. 'Did you see Christ?' Gerard asked. 'Yes', Fred replied. 'He was sitting upright on a straight-backed chair, clothed in a white robe, a staff in his hand, a crown of thorns on his head, looking disapproving.' If Fred was asked before taking part in the meditation about his basic notion of God and Christ, he would probably have said something like 'God is the God of love, mercy and compassion.' Yet his private 'feel' of God was clearly quite different. As he reflected on his inner picture of God he began to understand a lot more about his life: his disapproval of merriment, his unceasing attention to 'good works', the secret, tyrannical Christ in his mind who didn't allow him the simple pleasures of life. As Gerard Hughes says, Fred was suffering from 'a hardening of the oughteries'.

We all see God differently – and that's good. One helpful outcome of the Enneagram is the realization that different personality types each see the face of God in a different light or from a different perspective. One may be more aware of the caring side of God; another will feel God's joyfulness and adventure, another will be strongly conscious of divine justice, and so on.

And the same is true of different cultures: African, Asian and European eyes will each see God differently. In my Brethren Church I was taught that God is 'the perfect gentleman' – i.e. the quintessential, middle-class Englishman. And if by that we mean that God respects our humanity, that he treats people courteously and with grace, then we must surely agree. But if we confuse Christianity with Englishness, then we have transformed God into a monster. If there is a place for Christian mission in a post-colonial world, it certainly cannot be based on the enculturation of different peoples with a vision of the divine that is alien to who and what they are as people.

But there's a world of difference between varying healthy visions of God rooted in culture and personality and the distorted images of God that often take root in our subconsciousness, inflicting on us feelings of guilt or shame or even self-hatred. There's a huge difference between *feeling* as though God is an unforgiving bully, and *feeling* him as a caring, protective mother weasel, or a hen gathering her brood under her wings.

The reasons for our distorted images of God are varied and complex. Some can be rectified through sound teaching; some may require the help of a therapist. But to some extent we all need to discover healthier images of God. And one of the prime ways in which that happens is through community and relationships. Someone once said that God is a verb, not a noun. God is not a theological formula, a dogma, a credal statement or metaphysical entity. God is the flowing of life, a fellowship of love and communion. When we give and receive love, God is present. St John hits the nail right on the head: 'God is love, and those who abide in love abide in God, and God abides in them.' The Church is called to be the place where that sort of love is known and experienced. Sometimes it lives up to its calling; often, it doesn't.

So, God is not that inner voice which constantly says, 'That's not quite good enough.' He's the voice that says, 'Beloved, you are accepted. Go in peace.' God is not the abusive bully, the disapproving parent, or the petty policeman; and he's not the saccharine Santa Claus who showers you with gifts and then disappears. God is the hen with big wings, the little weasel who won't abandon you, even if she knew how.

Big souls

John 12.1–8

Without wishing to reveal too much about my personal pro-
clivities, I can tell you quite categorically that I am not a foot
man! I have never really 'got it' where feet are concerned. I
never look at a person and think, 'Phoooor! Nice pair of
feet.'

Of course, those of you who are foot connoisseurs will no
doubt point out that it all depends on the pair of feet in question. And yes, it's true: feet do vary. Some are petite and
pretty, others are just great plates of meat. Some are perfectly
formed, others are gnarled and lumpy. Some smell fresh as a
mountain stream, while others should definitely not be taken
out in public for fear of causing bystanders to collapse in a
coma.

But we're at that time of year again, that time in the church
calendar, when feet are paraded in public. Maundy Thursday
is the day when some churches hold a service of foot washing, in accord with the words of Jesus that we should wash
one another's feet. Sometimes it's done with an air of piety,
other times with great hilarity. It is almost always embarrassing.

At our foot-washing service a few years ago I gave everyone a surprise with my feet. We were sitting in a circle, with
a bowl of water and a towel being passed around. At the
given point we awkwardly removed one another's socks and

got down to some serious foot washing. I had prepared myself for the occasion – by painting my toe nails bright red! Imagine my foot-washer's shock as he pulled my sock off. I think it's safe to say that my pedicurial preparation helped banish any lingering embarrassment we all might have felt that night.

It has certainly always struck me as strange that a ceremony as embarrassing as foot washing could take place in the respectable context of an Anglican service. At a service of ordination a few years ago, where there were only two candidates for ordination – two women – it was gloriously weird to witness the Bishop of Salisbury remove his chasuble, take a bowl of water, tie a towel around his waist, and wash the two women's feet. Given the controversy that still surrounds the ordination of women priests, that was a powerful gesture for a senior bishop to perform.

But what happened in the little house in Bethany in John's Gospel took embarrassment to a whole new level, for several reasons. It was the home of Lazarus and his two sisters Mary and Martha. Picture it. It's a dinner party in honour of a special guest: their dear friend, Jesus, who had recently raised Lazarus from the dead. The house is probably filled with family, servants and friends.

Everything is going swimmingly. The food is plentiful and good. Their best wine is flowing freely. Everyone is enjoying the warm and stimulating conversation that always surrounded Jesus on these occasions. And then Mary does it. After disappearing for a while; she returns with a huge jar of very expensive perfume. Spikenard was a fragrant ointment derived from an aromatic herb found in the Himalayas. It is mentioned in the erotic context of the Song of Songs, where it gives fragrance to the king's couch. And its value was equal to a year's wages for the average working person.

To everyone's amazement, Mary begins to anoint Jesus' feet with the perfume. This is a deeply sensuous event. The

entire house is heavy with the wonderful smell of the ointment. And Mary, who, as a woman, would be forbidden to
even touch a man in public, lovingly massages Jesus' feet
with the spikenard. Then she loosens her hair, and wipes his
feet with it.

For those present this was a disturbing experience. It was
strangely erotic. It was extravagant and wasteful – Judas
points out how many poor people could be fed with the
money spent on this perfume. It was unconventional, embarrassing, discomforting, excessive, intimate and carnal –
enough to make most of us squirm. And, worse still, Jesus
went along with it. If this happened today, the Internet would
be heaving with outraged reactions from conservative Christian groups, calling for Jesus' resignation.

There are lots of theological undertones to the story. Let
me highlight two. First of all, John, the writer, has a much
more oblique and mysterious way of conveying his message
than the other Gospel writers. Clearly he wants to affirm that
Jesus is the Christ of God – the anointed one (that is what
'Christ' means – anointed). But what an amazing way to go
about doing it. Jesus' true identity is uncovered through an
outrageous and extravagant act, tinged with the erotic, performed by a woman.

Jesus himself brings another undertone to the surface,
when he says that Mary performed the act for his burial. It's
fascinating that the story of Jesus' ministry in the Gospel is
framed by two intuitive responses of women. At the marriage
at Cana, his mother, Mary, prompts him to perform his first
public miracle, even when he appears reluctant to do so.
Then here, another Mary instinctively anoints him for the
burial that will follow all too soon.

But what about the theological problem raised by Judas?
'Why was this perfume not sold for three hundred denarii
and the money given to the poor?' Motives are everything
here. Judas said this, we are told, not because he cared about

the poor, but because he was a thief, who kept the common purse and used to steal what was put into it. And like so many situations, this is not a simple matter of either/or. To force an either/or, for example between the aesthetics of worship – commissioning a triptych – and overseas aid is quite wrong, in my view.

Mary Gordon's novel *Final Payments* gives an interesting angle on this. At a critical point in the story, a memory of this passage from John is triggered in the mind of the protagonist. Suddenly she understands it in a new light, as the comments of Jesus illumine the sad waste she has been making of her life. In a moment she is awakened to herself. Jesus' words about the permanence of the poor and his own transience had always justified in her mind the excesses of centuries of exploitation. But now she says:

> I understand. What Christ was saying, what he meant, was that the pleasure of that hair, that ointment, must be taken. Because the accidents of death would deprive us soon enough. We must not deprive ourselves, our loved ones, of the luxury of extravagant affections. We must not second-guess death by refusing to love the ones we loved in favour of the anonymous poor.

Such observations will not remove our discomfort at the bizarre disparities of our world and neither should they. But there is no reason to make this into an either/or choice.

Perhaps our real unease with this story comes from our awkwardness in asking, receiving or giving blessings to each other at all. Expressions of love, nowhere near as extravagant as Mary's, are too vulnerable, too revealing of feeling, desire, or love.

Blessing like Mary is not an easy thing to do. It's much easier to resent extravagance like Judas – and it feels so much more justified. I've been thinking about the word 'magnanimous' – something Judas knew nothing of. Literally explained, 'magnanimous' means 'big souled'. At the risk of taking us back to feet, I'd like to say that one of my dearest goals in life is to be big-souled.

How much the world needs big-souled people. If only we had a big-souled leader somewhere in the Middle East – Israeli or Palestinian. We naturally think of Nelson Mandela at this point, basically because there are so few leaders around like him. What an extravagant waste – 27 years locked away in a prison. I hear a 'Judas' muttering in the background: 'Think what Mandela might have achieved if he'd gone a different route; if he'd avoided prison by escaping to another country; if he had fought apartheid by some other means.' Thank God, Mandela didn't listen to such voices.

Rabbi Lionel Blue says that if he were to choose a religious virtue like you choose a chocolate out of a box, he would go for generosity of spirit – big soul-ness. He says that there are two approaches in trying to bridge the gap between God and ourselves. One is to try to grow towards God, become bigger ourselves, more God-sized. We become more magnanimous. The other is to make God smaller. We don't try to change ourselves. That is too demeaning. We try to change the nature of religion. God becomes the extension of our own prejudice, our own small-mindedness and meanness.

There is a common device in all religious fanaticism, Lionel Blue says, when nobody is willing to listen but everyone is ready to pronounce. It's easy to get so absorbed by the small print that the big print of 'generosity' is lost. The small print, however clever it is, then becomes only the funeral rites of a real religion, which once lived. He finishes with these words:

I have met many 'religious' people in the course of my life. A very few were genuine saints, quite a few were phony, and most, including me, were a mixture of both. How do I distinguish the true from the false? Ideology isn't much use for such a basic question. The only testimonial I looked for was generosity.

Life is all about choices. We can't always get them right. But we can try to err on the right side. Mary teaches us to err on the side of generosity – big soul-ness – even if it is sometimes embarrassing, awkward, vulnerable, costly, dangerous.

Dear God, help us to be big-souled, daring, extravagant.

Symbol of passion

Philippians 2:5–11; Luke 19:28–40

Some of us are old enough to remember clearly the 1980s – torn jeans, the Human League and Maggie Thatcher. It seems astonishing that even such a short time ago apartheid still held sway in South Africa, and the Berlin Wall still stood defiantly between the East and the West.

Back in the midst of that era, in 1982, a quite remarkable item hit the news. George Bush Sr, then vice president, was representing the US administration in the Kremlin at the state funeral of Leonid Brezhnev, former supreme leader of the Soviet Union. Obviously, the whole event was highly choreographed to acclaim the great splendour and power of the Soviet empire.

Brezhnev's widow stood motionless at the side of the coffin. Then, as the soldiers moved forward to close the coffin, to everyone's astonishment, Brezhnev's wife reached out her hand and silently made the sign of the cross over her husband's body. It's difficult to overstate the audacity of that gesture in the very heart of the most brutally atheistic state in human history; Christians had faced the gulags or even execution for identifying with the cross. Some applauded it as the most outrageous act of civil disobedience the Soviet authorities had witnessed; it was certainly courageous, but I am sure that more than anything else it was the loving act of a grieving widow, commending her husband into the hands of a loving and forgiving God.

The Gospel reading for Palm, or Passion, Sunday tells the story of Christ's triumphant entry into Jerusalem; but we know it is the road to his execution, the passion and the cross. But I am not going to concentrate here on the blood and gore of the historical crucifixion, as in Mel Gibson's controversial film, *The Passion of the Christ*. I would rather spend a few moments pondering the great symbol that the cross represents.

It never ceases to amaze and inspire me that the cross – a gallows – should be the central symbol of the Christian faith. The symbols of other religions – a six-pointed star, a crescent moon, a lotus – all suggest beauty. But the symbol of Christianity is an instrument of death, which powerfully communicates hope.

Alexander Solzhenitsyn, the Russian author who spent many years in the gulag, talks about the powerful hope of the cross. After long suffering in the work camp of Siberia, he fell into despair. Like other prisoners, he had worked in the fields day after day, in rain and sun, during summer and winter. His days were filled with back-breaking labour and slow starvation. On a particular day, the hopelessness of his situation became too much. He saw no reason to continue living, to continue fighting the system. He thought that the rest of his life was meaningless, since he would most likely die in this Siberian prison. His life made no difference in the world. So he gave up.

Laying his shovel on the ground, he slowly walked to a crude work-site bench and sat down. He knew that at any moment a guard would order him to stand up, and when he failed to respond, the guard would beat him to death, probably with his own shovel. He had seen it happen to many other prisoners.

As he waited, head down, he felt a presence. Slowly, he

lifted his eyes and saw an old, skinny prisoner squat down next to him. The man said nothing. Instead, he drew a stick through the ground at Solzhenitsyn's feet, tracing the sign of the cross. The man then stood up and returned to his work.

As Solzhenitsyn stared at the sign of the cross, his entire perspective changed. He knew that he was only one man against the all-powerful Soviet empire. Yet in that moment, he knew that there was something greater than the evil that he saw in the prison, something greater than the Soviet Union. He knew that the hope of all mankind was represented in that simple cross. And through the power of the cross, anything was possible. Solzhenitsyn slowly got up, picked up his shovel, and went back to work. Nothing had changed, yet everything had changed; deep inside, he received hope – from two crossed lines scratched into the earth.

And that is all there is to it, really – two lines that intersect each other. You can sex it up with beautifully intricate Celtic design, you can form it from gold or silver, or cover it with precious stones; you can place a figure on it or leave it plain; you can turn it into a masterpiece of art, or make a multi-million-dollar film about it; you can venerate it, pray with it, gesture with it or 'take it up daily'; but it is still only two lines that intersect. So why is it so potent? Why does it evoke such hope and imagination?

Like all symbols, the cross is multivalent – capable of being interpreted in many different ways. However, the thing that imbues it with such energy and potency is the historic story that fired it into our consciousness, and the belief that it reveals something, not only about the very heart of God, but also about the soul of humanity. In a unique way, this symbol of the cross actually mediates the power of sacrifice, the virtue of vulnerability, the wonder of strength revealed through weakness, the transforming energy of forgiveness, the all-engulfing reach of love. To embrace such things is to know salvation.

Throughout history there have been claims to possess the original cross or pieces of it. But the truth is, the cross has been reproduced a million times and will continue to be reproduced. Countless physical crosses exist, each of which, in its own way, can mediate the vulnerable love that is the very heart of the cosmos.

One of the crosses in our church is the holocaust cross, made especially for St Luke's. This cross is formed of wood from a railway sleeper that carried thousands of Jews to their deaths in Auschwitz, and stone from a gas chamber. Yet the burden of the trains borne by this sleeper cannot compare with the weight of love it now communicates – a crucified God sharing in human pain and misery.

I also have a lovely Celtic stone cross, shaped by a disabled artist and given to me on my ordination – a sacrament of determination in the face of suffering and disadvantage. My father was disabled, so this cross conveys something very special to me.

But the sign of the cross is available to all of us, even when we have no object in our hands. That superstitious little practice of crossing one's fingers was originally a sign of the cross, a bodily prayer to Christ. And here at St Luke's I have noticed that increasing numbers of people use the sign of the cross as part of worship.

Because it is a symbol, crossing oneself can mean various things. Basically, it's a non-verbal prayer. We've all seen footballers (Italians in particular) crossing themselves as they come on to the pitch. You may say it's superstitious, but it's just their way of reaching out for help beyond themselves. It's no more superstitious than saying a prayer like: 'Dear God, help me to do my best, and keep me from injuring or being injured. Amen.' But the great thing about a symbolic prayer is that it is much more instinctive, and transcends words.

Mind you, things like this *can* be merely superstitious. I recall a comical example of this that I witnessed on the way to a funeral. If you have ever travelled in a funeral cortège you will probably have seen people crossing themselves as the hearse passes by. On this occasion I noticed a woman riding in the opposite direction on a bike. Clearly, her religious sensibility would not allow her to pass a funeral without crossing herself. The problem was, she was on her bike, and if she had stopped first, the funeral would have already passed her by. So she lunged into a hasty gesture, which made her wobble, and the next thing, I saw her collapsing on to the pavement with her bike. And I wasn't the only person to see what went on. I heard one of the family in the back of the car say: 'Jesus! Did you see that woman fall off her bike?' – which I'm sure was also a prayer on his part.

The practice of crossing oneself goes back to the early days of the Church. It's mentioned in the writings of Tertullian in the second century:

> In all our travels and movements; in all our coming in and going out, in putting on of our shoes, at the bath, at the table, in lighting our candles, in lying down, in sitting down, whatever employment occupies us, we mark our foreheads with the sign of the cross.

If, like me, it's not really part of your tradition, give it a go some time. And in case you're not sure: head – heart – left shoulder – right shoulder.

But in a very real sense, the sign of the cross is everywhere, all around us in this world. Wherever there is weakness, suffering or vulnerability, Christ is present. Here is a short anecdote from G. A. Studdert Kennedy, a great man who served as a chaplain in the trenches of the First World War. Through his experiences he became a passionate pacifist, and he was widely known as 'Woodbine Willie', because of his practice of giving the sacrament of a last cigarette to dying soldiers.

On June 17th 1917, I was running to our lines half mad with fright, though running in the right direction, thank God, through what had been a wooded copse. It was being heavily shelled. As I ran I stumbled and fell over something. I stopped to see what it was. It was an undersized, underfed German boy, with a wound in his stomach and a hole in his head. I remember muttering, 'You poor little devil, what had you to do with it? Not much great blond Prussian about you.' Then there came light. It may have been my imagination, but that does not mean that it was not also a reality, for what is imagination is often the road to reality. It seemed to me that the boy disappeared and in his place lay the Christ upon his cross, and cried, 'Inasmuch as you have done it to the least of these little ones you have done it unto me.' From that moment on I never saw a battlefield as anything but a crucifix. From that moment on I have never seen the world as anything but a crucifix.

May we have eyes to see and ears to hear the sufferings of Christ in our day-to-day world.

In the name of the Father and the Son and the Holy Spirit.

'The worst things are not the last things'

Acts 10.34–43; John 20.1–18

I read recently that the Twin Towers of the World Trade Center weighed a billion tonnes each, and that the weight of them falling caused an earthquake measuring 2.8 on the Richter scale. Many other buildings collapsed due to the reverberations, of course, and the NASDAQ building is now tilted four degrees off true vertical.

Just south of Tower Two stood St George's Greek Orthodox Church. It was a four-storey, 60-foot landmark. But when Tower Two collapsed on to the church, St George's was instantly compacted to a mere two feet. The pressure was so great that the church's iron safe apparently crumbled into dust and has never been found.

That's an amazing metaphor for what the followers of Jesus felt after his crucifixion. They had staked everything on the belief that this man was indeed the Messiah, the one who would deliver Israel. And look what had happened – an ignominious execution, the brutal death of a dream.

It was such a short time ago that they had sat around the table with him, laughing and telling stories, eating, and drinking rich red wine in the warmth and conviviality of that upper room. How they must, now, have remembered that weird bit in the middle of the meal, around the time that

Judas mysteriously disappeared, when Jesus enigmatically held up a loaf of bread and a glass of wine and talked about them as if they were his body and blood. It *was* a short time ago, yet it seemed that an eternity separated them from it now.

And what about the hellish confusion of the garden – one minute all was quiet; and Jesus was praying with Peter, James and John with the other disciples a short distance away. Then Judas reappeared with some very nasty people, and before they knew what was happening the disciples were scattered. Mark gives an almost comic account of one young disciple who only escaped by wriggling out of his clothes while the soldiers had hold of him, and running away naked and terrified. They were all on the run that day. But as they stood with the crowd watching as their friend Jesus was nailed to the tree, they must have felt like St George's Church, emotionally and spiritually crushed by a billion tonnes of rubble.

Then Sunday quietly dawned. With her heart flattened, Mary Magdalene crept through the darkness, hoping to offer one last expression of her love to Jesus, the man who had once healed her and who had given her a new life. But what she found was not what she had expected.

In a scene reminiscent of the Garden of Eden, Mary encountered the risen Christ. He still visibly carried the marks of his brutal death, but he was miraculously alive. More specifically, he had been re-created when the Spirit of God moved over the chaos of the crucifixion and the tomb, and brought new life into its bleak emptiness. Christ is risen! Christ is risen indeed.

I'm writing another book at present, about what I call 'second innocence'. The basic premise is quite simple: the faith journey begins with a wide-eyed innocence; we then pass through a period of disenchantment, when things seem to fall apart; but if we hang in we can move through to a second innocence, a moment of re-enchantment. St Luke's has been for me a place of re-enchantment – I was disillusioned with church leadership, and I certainly didn't see myself as a vicar – but hey . . . !

But this 'second innocence' thing offers a useful way of seeing what the disciples went through. Their three years of following Jesus around was their original innocence. They were great days – seeing the sick come by the truckload and go away healed; listening to Jesus' incredible teachings, half of which they didn't understand, but it was wonderful; and then watching him stuff the self-righteous Pharisees and tie the smart-Alec scribes in knots with their own arguments. The disciples believed anything was possible with Jesus – Romans? What Romans?

Then it all unravelled: the betrayal, the arrest, the farce of a trial, the beatings and the crucifixion. Talk about disenchantment – it was absolutely devastating. Everything they had hoped for and dreamed of was hammered to that cross, and died before their very eyes. But you know, as the old preacher said: 'It's Friday. But Sunday's coming!' Or to put that another way: 'The worst things are never the last things!'

This last statement comes from Frederick Buechner, a favourite American writer of mine. In a very moving account in his book *Listening to Your Life*, Buechner talks about the despair his father experienced during the Great Depression. He was a bright Princeton graduate but there was no work of any kind to be found, and sadly he turned to drink for comfort. One cold November morning in 1936, seeing no possible light on the horizon, he got up early, dressed, went down to the garage, carefully closing the door, and he turned on the ignition of the old Chevrolet, sat down on the running board, and was asphyxiated before anyone else got up.

For years Buechner told people his dad had died of 'heart trouble', which he now says was partially true – he had a heart, and it was troubled. Despite the hardship that followed his father's death, Buechner ended up following his dad into Princeton and became a successful writer. But then he found himself going through a time of deep despair, in a sustained period of writer's block. Eventually he found himself in Madison Avenue Presbyterian Church in New York, where he heard the English minister George Buttrick speaking. In the middle of the sermon Buechner had a religious epiphany, a profound sense that there is something beyond us upon which we can rely.

Buechner became a deep believer in God and he speaks of discovering a vital theme in the scriptures: that with God, the seemingly worst things were never the last things. To Buechner, God appeared as an ingenious alchemist, one who could take lead and transmute it into gold. This not only gave him an entirely fresh slant on his father's death – believing that death does not have the last word – it also gave him a perspective on his own life.

For Mary Magdalene and the disciples, things couldn't have got any worse; but it was then, in the midst of their profound disenchantment, that a moment of unexpected re-enchantment appeared in the resurrection – it was a second innocence.

Let me tell you about a more modern-day Mary Magdalene. Actually, let me ask you a question: when was the first woman ordained as a priest in the Anglican Church? Believe it or not, it was during the Second World War, in 1944. Florence Li Tim-Oi was a deacon caring for a congregation in a part of the diocese of Hong Kong that was cut off through the fighting. There was no way that a priest could get to them to administer the sacraments, for which they longed. So the bishop, Ronald Hall, decided to confirm what he was sure the Holy Spirit had already ordained, by making Florence a priest in the Church of God. The move was welcomed in the diocese, and Florence's congregation were overjoyed. But when news of it spread at the end of the war, a storm of protest arose around the world. Florence decided that the bishop's position was more important than hers, so she complied with the demand for her to give up her licence to work as a priest – though she never gave up her priestly orders.

It must have been like a death for Florence: a Good Friday experience, which she thought would never end. But the worst things are never the last things. In 1984, a celebration of Florence's fortieth anniversary of being ordained priest was held in Toronto, where women were now serving as priests. Surrounded by over 50 women priests, hundreds of deacons and 11 male bishops, Florence's priesthood was finally resurrected. She served as a priest until her death in 1992.

So how about you? Do you have precious dreams tucked away that you have lost hope of ever seeing fulfilled, and yet you just can't let go of them? Easter is a time of renewed hope. Have you experienced some dark night of the soul, a season of doubt and despair that you thought would never end? Have you felt the power of grief over the loss of someone precious to you; grief about some hope deferred, a youth that will never return, a life that, so far, hasn't turned out the way it was supposed to? Listen: the worst things are never the last things. Christ is risen!

Just before he died in 1965, Winston Churchill was asked to give the commencement address at a college. He was very old and had to be helped to the podium. They say he was so tottery that they weren't sure he would have strength enough to speak. At last he raised the head that had called Britain back from the brink, and said to the graduating students, 'Never, never give up.' And with that he turned around and sat down. It is probably the only commencement address in history that's been remembered verbatim by everybody who heard it.

Churchill apparently requested two things for the end of his funeral service. After the final benediction, he wanted one bugler to play 'Taps', the music that marks the end of the day. The 'Reveille', the wake-up call, was to follow this immediately. It would seem that Churchill believed that the worst things are never the last things, and the final sounds of history will not be 'Taps' but 'Reveille'.

Churchill, Buechner, the disciples, Mary Magdalene and saints throughout history all tell us that we must never, never give up, because who can tell what this God, who can make the things that are out of the things that are not, and can make dead things come alive again, might still be able to do with any difficult situation. Bet your life on it. The seemingly worst things are never the last things with this alchemist God. God always has something creative up his sleeve. The empty tomb is our basis of hope and for never, never giving up. The worst things are never the last things.

The unfinished story

Acts 10.34–43; Mark 16.1–8

I watched a film a couple of weeks ago that was the biggest pile of tosh I had experienced for some time. It was *The Perfect Storm*, a tale about a bunch of fisherman, led by George Clooney, who, faced with the choice, decide to sail right through the perfect storm, rather than avoid it, which they could have done. Not surprisingly, they all perish. And that's that – end of film. Great!

However, the worst thing about this film wasn't that they all died – sometimes stories have to have a sad ending. No, the worst thing was that I really didn't care whether they died or not. Indeed, I was quite glad that this bunch of losers drowned in the ocean of their own ridiculous machismo.

But some stories do have truly sad endings and you desperately wish that they could end differently. Both Pat and I get very emotional when it comes to sad endings. But of the two of us I'd say that Pat probably deals with them better than me. The reason is simple: if she doesn't like an ending she just makes up a different one – an amazing talent which I wish I possessed.

Actually, most stories can be told – and finished – in a number of different ways. It depends on who is telling the story, what they are feeling when they tell the story, and what, if anything, they are trying to convey in the telling of the story. And if you want to be really trendy you can get into what's known as reader-response theory and say that it will also depend on the thoughts, feelings and experiences of those listening to the story.

All of which brings me to the way the four evangelists choose to end their stories, the Gospels. Each of the endings is quite different. And Mark's ending is the most different of all – partly because, as usual, he is briefer and more terse than the others, but also because he finishes on such a disturbing note. In fact, compared with the others, it's an unfinished story. But perhaps that is the point.

Each of the other Gospels finishes on a high: Jesus appears in various ways to the disciples, who are transported from doubt to faith and recognize their mission to get out there and tell the world about Jesus. Mark ends with the two Marys fleeing from the empty tomb in great fear, unable to speak to anyone about what they have seen.

Now that isn't exactly a high note to finish on – distinctly lacking in spin, if you ask me. Although, if you check your Bible, you might want to take issue with me. You might say, 'Hang on a minute, Dave, verse 8 isn't the end of the chapter; there are another 12 verses after that, and it finishes like the other Gospels, with the disciples going out and proclaiming the message.' But, you see, it has long been known that these 12 verses weren't written by Mark; they are the work of an editorial spin-doctor who, much later on, decided to give the story a better finish.

Personally, I really like the way Mark ends his Gospel. It is as if he is saying, 'Look, this is the beginning of a journey and not the destination. If you want to find the risen Christ, you're going to have to carry on searching yourself. No one here is going to give you a nice little "happy ever after", or a neatly pre-packaged set of certainties. You're going to have to risk everything on the adventure just like the rest of us.' And that's what faith is, folks: it's an adventure, not a destination.

Think about these women, the two Marys: two faithful women who could hardly wait for the Saturday Sabbath to be over. At dawn they appear at the tomb with their precious burial spices. They aren't looking forward to dealing with that huge stone over the entrance. They are still in a daze of confusion and grief. Yet, as they approach the tomb, they realize that the stone is already moved. And there, sitting calmly just inside the entrance, is a mysterious young man, dressed in a white robe. They are 'alarmed', Mark says. You bet they are. Their thoughts run riot as they feel the cool air of the tomb engulf them. Who is this man? What is he doing there? And where is Jesus?

Then the young man (angel?) makes one of the most famous statements of all time: 'He is not here.' Interesting, isn't it? He doesn't say, 'He's risen. He's here.' He says, 'He's risen. He's *not* here.' Interesting because the churches have a tendency to say, 'Christ is here . . . we've got an exclusive . . . we've cornered this particular market . . . if you want to find Christ, you're going to have to come to us.' But the angel says, 'Christ is risen. He's not here. And you're going to have to get out there and find him.' You see, it's an adventure.

Actually you could say that these two statements – 'he is here' and 'he is not here' – symbolize two quite different approaches to Christian faith. One is preoccupied with having answers to all of life's questions, the other realizes that answers are not always available. The first is taken up with arrival, the other relishes the fact that the adventure has just begun. One likes to tie up loose ends, the other is much more comfortable with the sense of life's mysteries.

I remember coming across a man some years ago who claimed to have cracked the divine code in the Bible. He actually said that there was now no question about the Christian faith that he could not answer. 'Once you understand the principles,' he claimed, 'you needn't be in the dark about anything. Jesus Christ is the light, so nothing need now be hidden.' Resisting the temptation to remind him about two small parts of the male anatomy, I simply responded by saying that he clearly worshipped a different God from me. The God I am absorbed with cannot be codified, formularized, pinned down, or boxed in by human reason; the Christ of resurrection is wild, undomesticated, elusive and mysterious. Understanding him is an adventure that will take us far beyond death.

I think this is what the two women were confronted with when they approached the empty tomb. They were emotionally battered and bereaved, but they thought they knew what to expect. Dead saviours are a sad affair but at least you know what to do with them: honour them with perfumes and spices, tell stories about the wonderful things they did, and build impressive shrines in their memory. But a risen Saviour who enigmatically disappears and re-emerges in mysterious circumstances, who can be pursued but never apprehended – now that is a different kettle of fish altogether.

Mark's 'unfinished' Gospel story is very clear that Christ did indeed rise from the dead, but I think it is also saying that if anyone thinks that the resurrection brings easy answers to hard questions or difficult and painful situations, they are very mistaken. And yet the triumphalist message is preached in many churches: if you only believe, you can be healed; if you have faith, God will deliver you from your financial problems, your relationship difficulties, your aches and pains, etc. God only knows the damage such simplistic teaching creates.

I believe in the resurrection of Christ as an invitation to live with holy zeal, not as an escape from death. I believe in the resurrection of Christ as an invitation to embrace the mystery of life, not as an escape from the need to wrestle with faith. I believe in the resurrection of Christ as an invitation to live the incarnational life – to allow God to live in and through us – not as a rejection of the earthly body. I believe in the resurrection of Christ as a living symbol of God's perpetual creativity, as a proclamation of that mystery at the centre of our existence. Most of all, I believe in the resurrection of Christ as the infusion of divine energy that always brings forth a new beginning. Resurrection says that there are always new opportunities, always second chances.

There is one more thing we should notice in the story. The angel tells the women that Jesus is not there, but he does give them a forwarding address: 'He is going ahead of you to Galilee.' Easter faith is not about pinning Christ down, but it is about pointing us where to go next in order to keep following him on the great divine adventure. Go to Galilee. Of course, Galilee wasn't a strange place to the women. It was where they lived. It was their ordinary life. And yet it would never be entirely ordinary again. The Easter message is that Christ is not contained in special buildings, religious activities or Sunday-best behaviour. Christ is in your Galilee, waiting to reveal your ordinariness in a whole new light.

Being a Christian means embarking on an adventure, the divine adventure. It's an unfinished story, waiting for us to write the next chapter. On Easter morning we are invited to follow the ancient tradition of renewing our baptismal commitment, a commitment not to a set of doctrines or principles, however important they may be, but to an adventure. Go to Galilee, knowing that Christ is there already waiting for you.

Let me end with a few wise and inspiring words from the poet Rainer Maria Rilke:

Have patience with everything unresolved in your heart
and try to love the questions themselves
as if they were locked rooms or books written in a very
    foreign language.
Don't search for the answers,
which could not be given to you now,

because you would not be able to live them.
And the point is to live everything.
Live the questions now.
Perhaps then,
someday far in the future,
you will gradually,
without even noticing it,
live your way into the answers.

It's all a matter of trust

Psalm 23; John 10.22–30

I met Karen through taking her partner's funeral. Phil was 43. He collapsed and died of a heart attack outside Pentonville Prison. He was out running to keep fit. Karen and Phil had been together for almost ten years. He sounded like a great guy. Karen told me that he couldn't pass a *Big Issue* seller on the street without buying a copy; she'd known him buy as many as seven copies in one week. When she teased him about being 'a big soft-headed bugger', he'd always say that it could have been him sleeping rough on the streets.

Karen was devastated by her loss. I normally spend about 20 or 30 minutes with people planning their loved one's funeral, but I was with her for two hours. She had no idea how she was going to make it through the funeral. When the day arrived, she looked like a tightly wound spring, determined to hold it all together. Her worst moment was going to be when I hit the button for the coffin to disappear. She dreaded it, but made the wise decision (I think) to see her way through the ordeal rather than just leave the coffin in the chapel. As it happens, she dealt with the whole event courageously – weeping but not turning away. Afterwards I asked her how she had coped. Her reply surprised me, though it probably shouldn't have. 'It was when you read the twenty-third psalm, Dave. I'm not sure that I followed any of the words, but a great peace came over me as you read it. And I knew I could make it through.'

You probably know that Psalm 23 sung to the tune 'Crimond' is top of the funeral hymn hit parade. It's been there for as long as anyone can remember, and it's likely to go on that way. But why do people find it so helpful in times of grief and loss? Karen gives us one important clue. She said, 'I'm not sure I followed any of the words.' In other words, the psalm comforted her in a symbolic way, rather than through the wise words of which it is undoubtedly comprised. Symbols operate in what's called a gestalt fashion – their force lies in the impact of the whole rather than through the individual parts. It's not just what it says that is important, it is also what it signifies – trust in one who cares.

We do well to remember that, first and foremost, the twenty-third psalm is a song, a poem, a piece of art. It is profoundly theological, but it isn't couched in theological language. Its 15 lines are packed with pictures and images – green pastures, dark valleys, a table of good things, anointing oil, a cup running over. No rational arguments are offered: no explanations for pain and suffering; no cheering answer to the agonizing 'Why?' that rumbles in the minds of the bereaved. The psalm just doesn't work on that level. It talks in the language of right-brain rather than left-brain consciousness.

But Psalm 23 is also powerful because it connects us to a tradition. When we speak it or sing it we enter a dance. It's a dance that lots of people who request Psalm 23 at a funeral hardly ever take part in ('We're not really churchgoers, vicar,' people say to me repeatedly), yet, even though they're rusty on the steps, they still want to be reminded of the dance in times of heartache and pain. It's a bit like the effect of hearing a well-known carol near Christmas, or passing through familiar streets on your way home after a long trip away – deep resonances are aroused.

So when yet another family requests the twenty-third

psalm at the funeral of their loved one, I am not surprised. And believe it or not, I never tire of helping them to sing or say it, because I know that this little poem – not the best that was ever written, by a long chalk – can connect them in some magical way to their loved ones, and to a God who surrounds them and holds them up in their grief.

However, it is regrettable if Psalm 23 is associated solely with death and funerals. It's really a song of life. It also teaches us about the nature of faith in every situation in life. For many people today, faith means believing certain things – giving mental assent to particular propositions about God. But is this actually what faith is about? Does salvation really hinge on one believing the 'right things'? Can God truly be bothered about what we manage to believe in our heads? I think not. This idea of faith owes more to post-Enlightenment rationalism than to the teachings of scripture. With more than a touch of irony St James warns: 'You believe that God is one; you do well. Even the demons believe – and shudder.'

Faith is not about belief; it's about trust. It's not about believing statements *about* God, but about trusting *in* God. The image often conjured up is that of swimming or floating on water. Due to a childhood illness, I only learned to swim in my early twenties. And I thought I would never get the hang of it. As soon as I was out of my depth I would tense up and start thrashing around, and I'd sink. The breakthrough came on the north Cambrian coast where, at last, I learned to lie on my back and trust the water to hold me up. It's so simple, yet it can be so hard to do.

It follows, of course, that the opposite of faith is not doubt or disbelief, but anxiety and worry. Not that this makes *me* feel any better – sometimes I feel as though I've turned worry into an art form! But the message of Jesus is clear: 'Do not worry, do not be anxious.' This is good news, indeed. Imagine a life free from worry and anxiety, and you have imagined a life of faith, a life of trust.

Psalm 23, then, is a song of trust. Or as someone put it, 'an ode of trust and confidence in God'. Rabbi Harold Kushner presents it as a three-act play depicting a person's life story. First there is peace and serenity, then darkness and grief, and finally a return to peace.

Kushner knows what he is talking about. He is well known for his best-selling little book, *Why Bad Things Happen to Good People*, in which he tells the story of Aaron, his son who died of a rare and incurable disease at the age of 14. Prior to Aaron's death, Kushner enjoyed a marvellous life as a popular parish rabbi in Boston. But his son's illness changed everything and forced him to enter his own 'valley of the shadow of death'. His vision of a God who looked after everything, ensuring that good things happen to good people, was shattered. But he rediscovered God in a new way: a God who won't necessarily make nasty things go away, but who will always be with you when the nasty things happen. Some bad things happen, he says, because God gave human beings free will; some arise from the random process of nature; some are just bad luck.

To return to Harold Kushner's three-act play approach to Psalm 23: Act One is the picture of initial serenity. The psalmist begins with an understanding that the Almighty is friendly. God loves us. He's on our side. That's pretty basic to a Christian vision of God, yet it's amazing how many people struggle with negative images of God. Albert Einstein famously said that science could teach us much about the universe, but that it was useless at answering the most important question of all: is the universe a friendly place? The psalmist gives an unequivocal answer: The Lord is my shepherd – the universe is sustained by one who undertakes to care for me. He provides what is needed. He leads and guides me. His surrounding presence brings peace and stillness.

Act One is about trust in good times – when we feel secure, when we sense that life is good; when we eat and drink in the company of friends and family, when the future feels hopeful. Some years ago I came across a quote from a former Christian who is now an atheist. He said that the thing he missed most as an atheist was having somewhere to focus his feelings of gratitude when life felt good.

Then comes Act Two. The road leads away from the green pastures, the still waters and the pleasant paths. The skies become grey, the road gets bumpy, and you find yourself in a dark valley of grief and loss. The good life of Act One disappears into the distance. Perhaps it is indeed the death of a loved one that takes us down this road. But bereavement comes in many forms: a loss of good health, a terminated career, an experience of rejection or betrayal, a deeply felt regret over something you are now powerless to rectify, the passing of youth, a financial disaster. The joy of Act One is having someone to be grateful to in good times; the compensation in Act Two is having someone to cry out to in times of despair, perhaps even someone to direct your anger towards, someone whose love is not daunted by our negative emotions, whose compassion is not deterred by our accusations. But we find no miracle answers in the valley of darkness; no quick-fix solutions, just the pledge that God is with us. As Harold Kushner says, 'The most important lesson is that in times of trouble, God does not explain, God comforts.'

Finally, we come to Act Three. The disenchantment of Act Two gives way to a second naïvety, as we learn to trust again. I like the idea of a table prepared. Isn't it great when you arrive at a dinner party and see the table laid? Someone has bothered to prepare things for you. You are an honoured guest. This is precisely the case in our Eucharist: a symbolic meal awaits us, the foretaste of a heavenly banquet. In Act Three we are welcomed home. Home – a place of refuge and acceptance, a place where we can be ourselves, where there are no expectations, save that we love and care for those around us. I look forward to the heavenly house of the Lord, but meanwhile I'm very happy to be in his earthly house, this warm and friendly community.

Let me leave you with an image that encapsulates the spirit of Psalm 23. Walking on the Yorkshire moors on a freezing November day a couple of years ago, Pat and I noticed a sheep in distress. It had fallen into a hollow and was stuck on its back, completely unable to get back on its feet. I approached it, speaking calmly, trying to reassure it in sheepy language. It didn't panic or struggle. It was completely help-less and vulnerable, but it seemed to know that I wasn't going to hurt it. It was a pretty big animal, so I grabbed it firmly and pulled it back on to its feet. It paused for a moment, looking at me, and then peacefully walked away as though nothing had happened.

'He restores my soul.' Faith isn't about believing state-ments *about* God. It's about trusting *in* God. It's about allow-ing him to guide us, restore us, comfort us, feed us, anoint us – and most of all, befriend us.

The peace of the Lord be with you.

Two charcoal fires

Acts 9.1–6; John 21.1–19

Have you ever been caught out? I mean, really caught out? Ever said something awful about someone without realizing that they were standing right behind you? Ever been caught red-handed taking something that wasn't yours? Ever made a comment, not knowing that the microphone was still on? Worse still, have you ever let down someone you love, and then suddenly realized what you've done?

It was a cold night, and Peter huddled up to the charcoal fire with a bunch of others who were looking for a bit of warmth. This was a time when Peter didn't want to be recognized. He desperately didn't want to forsake Jesus, but he knew that his own life was at risk if he were seen. So he pulled his coat up high around his neck and tried to lie low. But, then, oh heck, why is that young woman looking at him? 'Don't I know you?' she asked. 'Aren't you a friend of this Jesus guy?'

'No, not me,' Peter replies.

Peter's feeling very lonely, and wonders where John has got to. The night seems even colder. Peter holds out his hands to warm them in front of the coals. Then a man standing near to the woman squints his eyes in the darkness, looking in Peter's direction. 'Yes, of course you're one of them; you've got a Galilean accent.'

'Look, mate,' Peter barks back, 'I've told you, I don't know what you're on about.'

Perhaps it was Peter's over-reaction, but now everyone is looking at him, and another man pipes up: 'Yes, I remember you. You were the mouthy one in his gang, the one I always thought was too big for his boots.'

Peter has had enough: 'Listen, I've told you, I have no idea what you're talking about, and you're really annoying me now. Just leave me alone, will you?'

'All right, mate, whatever,' the man mutters.

At that moment, there is the distant sound of a cockerel crowing. Then there is another, much closer, then another and another, until it seems to Peter that every cockerel in Jerusalem is crowing at the same time.

But time moves on. All of that seems an age ago. Now it's a misty grey morning just off the shore of the Sea of Galilee. Peter and his friends have been fishing all night without catching a thing. Maybe they've lost the knack – been listening to too many sermons instead of plying their trade. But then, in the fresh morning air there is a distinct whiff of charcoal burning nearby. It takes Peter right back to that wretched night, the night that he hated more than any other night. The night he was caught out. The night the microphone was left on, and everyone in heaven and earth heard him spew out curses on his best friend.

Who would have thought they were going to run into Jesus – there, on a deserted beach at the crack of dawn? The man they thought was dead. But there he was, large as life, cooking breakfast for them all. As Peter once again shuffled up to the charcoal fire, nervously munching the meal Jesus had set before them, he couldn't be sure whether his shivering was down to the chill in the air or the cold sweat he felt coming over him.

In the strange quiet that followed breakfast, Jesus points to the enormous catch of fish, the boats and the nets, and asks, 'Simon son of John, do you love me more than these?' Then, with the skill of a therapist and the compassion of a friend,

Jesus guides Peter through a powerful reversal of what took place around the other fire – three pledges of love for three excruciating and deeply regretted denials. It's what has been described as 'a recycling of denial into affirmation'. Over a sacramental breakfast on a quiet beach, Peter ran into the God of all grace, and was never the same again.

Peter's first charcoal fire was marked by fear, loneliness and betrayal, the second by forgiveness, friendship and the meal of a new beginning. It was a 'second innocence'. Not that things could ever go back to how they were. Peter's original innocence was shattered that chilly night in the garden, but grace would swallow up all guilt, and the adventure could continue.

Both the Bible readings are about conversion, about choices, and about running into God just when you least expect it. These two men, Peter and Paul, are the two most influential figures in the early church. Yet neither of them had a particularly good CV: one forsook Jesus in his hour of greatest need, the other was a crazy religious fanatic who tortured and murdered the followers of Jesus, believing he was doing God's will.

Isn't it fascinating that Jesus never once mentioned Peter's denial? He did not say, 'Listen, Peter, what went wrong? Why did you deny you even knew me? Why did you curse my very name?' Grace takes a different approach. Grace can put the past behind. Grace can create a new reality, a new future. Grace does not even ask 'Are you sorry?' but, 'Do you love me?'

There is always a second chance with God. I wonder if you recall the story in the press about Peter Hollingworth, who was forced to step down as Governor General of Australia because of accusations that he had mishandled allegations of clergy abuse when he was Archbishop of Brisbane. It was alleged that Hollingworth had covered up complaints of clergy sexual abuse and protected the offenders. And under a barrage of pressure he admitted he had got it wrong and resigned as Governor General.

This much was well reported in the media. What is less well known is that since his resignation Peter Hollingworth has devoted time and energy to understanding the nature and impact of sexual abuse. He has sought to face up to his critics, including those who were working with victims and survivors. And he has sought forgiveness from those he hurt.

One of Hollingworth's severest critics at the time was Barbara Biggs, who has written numerous books on child abuse (having been a victim herself), and is an advocate of other survivors. It says a lot for the Archbishop's 'conversion' that Biggs has now invited him to write the foreword to her new book, *The Road Home*. Needless to say, the media that hounded him for his resignation have said little about his reparations.

Thank God that an archbishop can find grace, just as the one named by the Catholic Church as the first pope found grace, and St Paul (the 'chief of sinners'), the great hero of the Evangelicals, also found grace. If we look at these men, and indeed at church leaders throughout history, we could say that the church is founded on failure or even sin – there's been plenty of it about. But we would be wrong. The church is founded on grace, forgiveness and reconciliation.

Peter's two charcoal fires really do take us to the heart of the matter. They represent two types of religion. The first is the religion of guilt. When we gather around this fire we can never escape our own cycle of failure. We know what we are supposed to say and how we should behave, but we just can't bring ourselves to do it. And we experience constant guilt about our failure. This is the religion of 'wretched me'. It's all about me – my willpower, my strenuous efforts, my failed goodness, my shame, my sense of rejection, my poor self-image.

The second fire symbolizes the religion of grace. When we gather around this fire, we know from the start that our acceptance is nothing to do with our efforts, our ability to overcome, our strength to do what is right. Here, we know that we have failed miserably, and we know that our failure is known and understood, but dealt with. Here, we do not feed on the fruits of our own efforts, however good they may be; here the meal is already prepared for us. Here, we can bring our sin, our denial, our betrayal of all we hold dear, and find it recycled into love and affirmation, and a constructive mission to care in God's name.

This fire is all about grace. When I baptized two lovely little children recently, I read from Psalm 139:

> O LORD, you have searched me and known me.
> You know when I sit down and when I rise up;
> you discern my thoughts from far away.
> You search out my path and my lying down,
> and are acquainted with all my ways.
> Even before a word is on my tongue,
> O LORD, you know it completely.
> You hem me in, behind and before,
> and lay your hand upon me.

No wonder David exclaims, 'Such knowledge is too wonderful for me.' David understands God as the all-seeing eye; the one from whom we can hide nothing. He's there on a cold night, when a dear friend is cursed and betrayed. He's there even when the microphone *is* turned off and no one can hear. Nothing slips by his constant gaze.

This is not the eye of judgement, rejection and disapproval, but the eye of compassion and grace. T. S. Eliot says that we are consumed by either fire or fire. Let's huddle around the fire of grace. Confess our sins. Acknowledge our failure. Feed his lambs. Eat the feast with gladness. It is with compassion that we are seen and judged.

Rumours of glory

Isaiah 6.1–8; John 3.1–17

There's a story about a man who was confined to a prison cell. His only view of the outside world was through a small window high up on the wall. To begin with he hated his confinement, and despised the miserable view he had on the outside world, which was the only world he believed in; it was also the world for which he longed.

But time passed, and that little window became his friend. Yes, it offered only tiny morsels of life – a wisp of cloud, a free-flying bird, a passing plane, a falling leaf, a raindrop, a snowflake – but he gradually came to see that this was not such a bad thing. It forced him to concentrate on the particular, and to imagine a lot from a little. Indeed, he was amazed at discovering how much of life can be found in one small sample.

At times the view from the window was shallow and opaque. The world seemed to end at the window. But at other times the window opened on to a blue and empty sky. Then it gave access to infinity, and he felt awakening within him transcendent longings he never knew were there. The little window offered glimpses of heaven as well as of earth.

When, eventually, the man was released, he found himself seeing everything in general and nothing in particular. And to his dismay, the sense of 'beyond' that he had caught sight of through the little window, the stirrings of a transcendent dimension to life, now began to diminish. Paradoxically, it seems that the sense of the transcendent is linked to an appreciation of the particular.

Trinity Sunday is the day when preachers around the world fling themselves into the task of explaining the mysteries of the Holy Trinity to bemused and sometimes semi-comatose congregations. And I'm not averse to the odd fling myself – the notion of the trinity, a social God, is pretty important to me, too. But perhaps we try too hard. Perhaps we're straining to see the big picture when what we should do is simply gaze with greater expectation through our little windows.

I don't suppose you could call Isaiah's window little – he had something more like a multi-screen panoramic vision of God: 'I saw the Lord sitting on a throne, high and lofty . . . Seraphs [angels] were in attendance above him. He even overheard the relentless angelic conversation: 'Holy, holy, holy is the LORD of hosts; the whole earth is full of his glory.' I like that: the whole earth is full of God's glory. What a massive, inclusive vision. Not the church full of God's glory, not St Paul's Cathedral, not St Peter's in Rome, but the whole earth – the whole earth is full of God's glory.

Sadly, few of us see it that way. We look out on grey mornings and see drizzly rain; we sit in lines of traffic or stand, half-asleep, on a jam-packed tube; we watch the news and see more burned-out buses in Israel, more crying babies in the aftermath of an explosion; we drudge our way through yet another daily round, dispose of another dirty nappy, bag our rubbish, find ourselves caught up in yet another grouchy exchange with a loved one.

The whole earth is full of God's glory – we wish!

Yet the little windows on the transcendent are still there, if only we can lift our eyes to see them. And I'm really taken with this idea that the way we encounter the transcendent is by concentrating on the particular. And that's another way of saying that God is found most profoundly in the ordinary things in life, the things we most take for granted.

In a wonderful book called *Mystical Passion: The Art of Christian Loving* William McNamara says that it's better to stay at home and smell a flower, bake an apple pie, or sweep a floor than to have a spooky, spurious religious experience at a prayer meeting. It's better to simply enjoy the sunshine or a good show than to meddle curiously and conceitedly with the occult. It's better to romp with the dogs in the back yard than to engage in haughty spiritual conversations at church, if the dogs in the yard help us to be less egoistical and more God-centred. I tell you, that's my kind of spirituality. How can we relish the higher things of God if we can't enjoy some simple little things like a glass of beer, a boat ride, a warm bath, a good kiss, a belly laugh, smelling the air after a shower of rain, lying in the sun, gazing into the soft brown eyes of a furry creature – all these things can be rumours of glory, tiny windows on the great beyond.

Take the film *American Beauty*. It's a fascinating delve into the modern American psyche, based around the story of Lester, the archetypal Mr Suburbia who's trying to regain his youth. In one beautifully shot scene Lester's daughter is with Ricky, her boyfriend, who says he wants to show her the most beautiful thing he ever found. It's a short film portraying a plastic bag being blown around by the wind just minutes before a snow storm. The image of the swirling bag is spell-binding. Ricky says, 'This bag was just dancing with me, like a little kid begging me to play with it.' He goes on to say that, sitting watching the bag, he realized that there is this entire life behind things, and this incredibly benevolent force that wanted him to know that there was no reason to be afraid, ever. The whole earth is full of God's glory. St Paul says, 'In him we live and move and have our being.'

'Sometimes', Ricky says, 'I feel there's so much beauty in the world I just can't take it, and my heart is just going to cave in.' I know what he means. But on the few occasions I've felt like that it has always been in response to something very particular – a tiny window on God, a rumour of glory. I felt it when I fell in love with my wife. And I felt it again when I watched two of my children being born and then held them in my arms – minute, yet perfectly formed, scraps of humanity – windows on God, rumours of glory.

It's amazing how many people's lives are transformed when they have a baby. Just this week I was listening to people calling Radio Five Live to talk about parenthood. It was particularly moving to hear guys who had worked in highly paid jobs in the City, who had given it all up to stay at home and look after their small children. Their whole value system and priorities had been turned upside down by becoming a parent. The transcendent made visible through a tiny window.

The Christian doctrine of the Holy Trinity springs out of a glorious affirmation that God is both beyond creation *and* revealed within it (transcendent and immanent). Jesus Christ is the 'beyond' come among us. In him we get the clearest glimpse of what God is like.

The tragedy is that all too often we have tried to contain Jesus within the Church – in doctrines, in the structures of formal religion, in theological formulas. We've invoked his name to oppress those who don't fit our mould, to exclude those we don't like or who don't believe the same things as we do. But he won't be tied down. You'll find him in the most unlikely places: hiding in a barn in ancient Palestine, smiling from the face of a baby in a supermarket, suffering in the broken bodies of AIDS sufferers, twinkling in the eye of an elderly woman about to slip away with dementia, grinning in the midst of a storm, serving us through the mundane acts of kindness by a loved one whom we take for granted.

These and many more things could be your little windows on God – your rumours of glory.

It's amazing how much of God can be found in one small sample of life.

Finding the child within

Mark 9.30–37

There was a little book published many years ago called *Children's Letters to God*. It was a collection of prayers written by children. Here are a few examples I can recall:

> Dear God, who does your job when you're on holiday?

> Dear God, did you mean to make the giraffe look like that, or was it an accident?

> Dear God, instead of letting people die and having to make new ones, why don't you just keep the ones you have now?

> Dear God, thank you for my baby brother, but what I prayed for was a puppy.

And my favourite:

> Dear God, are boys really better than girls? I know you are one, but try to be fair.

I have to confess to having more than the odd doubt as to whether *Children's Letters to God* was in fact written by children. But who cares? It's pretty entertaining anyway.

It's interesting that, instead of holding up an adult in front of a bunch of kids and saying, 'Children, learn to be adults,' Jesus lifts up a little child and says, 'Adults, learn to be like this.' It's particularly interesting since in Jesus' day children had virtually no status at all. In the eyes of the law they were well nigh invisible, having only the rights of a slave or a domestic animal. They were possessions, investments in the future, but they did not have any real significance or importance in and of themselves.

So it's all the more surprising that Jesus said so much about children, that he held them up as examples of how his kingdom works, and that he insisted on allowing mothers to bring their little ones to him to be blessed.

Jesus said, 'Whoever welcomes one such child in my name welcomes me, and whoever welcomes me welcomes . . . the one who sent me.' We can think about these words on two levels: first, in the obvious, literal sense that Jesus meant them.

Let me describe two real-life cameos involving children. The first took place some years ago at a conference I was speaking at. One of the other speakers, renowned for his great oratorical skills, was responding to a group of adoring 'fans' in the dining hall. After a short while his nine-year-old son sidled up with a simple request. It took some time for the boy's presence to be noticed. Then his dad pushed him aside several times, eventually telling him to go and ask his mother. He was far too busy for such trivial matters. I don't think the incident even registered with his fan club.

The second scene is in the Old Deanery, the residence of the Bishop of London. Pat and I had been invited to a dinner party in honour of Professor Raymond Brown, the distinguished Roman Catholic New Testament scholar. Unexpectedly, I was seated next to the great man, which I found a tad intimidating to begin with. But I soon relaxed. To our surprise the bishop's children brought the food to the table. And it soon became clear that Raymond Brown, a lifelong celibate whose entire life was spent in the academic world, was very comfortable with children. As the meal progressed, he was perfectly happy to turn away from the theological discussion to joke and play with the children. A little later, over coffee, Bishop Richard himself beckoned one of his children to come over and sit on his knee while the discussion continued. What a contrast to the other scene!

'Whoever welcomes one such child in my name welcomes me.' The underlying lesson is clear: you can tell a great deal about a person by the way they treat children. And clearly Jesus was a fun person to be around: children soon discern people's attitudes toward them. Johnny Cash, who died not long ago, made a very low-budget film back in the 1970s about the life of Jesus called *Gospel Road*. It wasn't a great production, but I still hold the images in my mind of Jesus splashing around in the water at the edge of the Sea of Galilee with a group of children.

The reason Jesus held up the child in today's story is plain to see. He and his followers had been on the road all day. Jesus had tried to explain why they were going to Jerusalem: it wasn't to seize power or set in motion a populist uprising against the authorities. He was going to be betrayed and face execution. The whole thing was too heavy for the disciples, so they skulked off and ended up in an argument as to who was the greatest among them. How embarrassing, we say, with impeccable hindsight. But, you know, I suspect that they were simply voicing the kind of thoughts we all have from time to time.

It's said that if you take any ten chickens, put them in a pen together and spread a little chicken feed about, in a matter of minutes the chickens, which were previously strangers, will establish a pecking order. Chicken number one will peck at and intimidate chicken number two; chicken number two takes it and then turns around and pecks at chicken number three. And the pecking order continues all the way down to chicken number ten, who needless to say has a pretty miserable existence: pecked, but with no one to peck.

The purpose of this profound biological observation is, I hope, pretty obvious: most of us feel a need to know where we stand in relationship to our peers. It's a natural reaction, and harmless enough, provided we know when to 'let it lie'.

Ambition isn't a bad thing per se. Indeed, it's a very important element in getting things done: imagine where we would be if people hadn't been ambitious and adventurous. What a bland, lifeless place the world would be. But this wasn't the level of the disciples' argument. Their ambition is the sort we need to grow out of as soon as possible – childish one-upmanship. In effect, Jesus says to them: 'Grow up, guys! Don't you see that it's the people who serve their neighbour who are truly great, not the ones who spend all their energy trying to get one over on them.' A true sense of self-worth and personal value stems not from individualism but from relationality.

'Whoever welcomes one such child . . . welcomes me, and whoever welcomes me welcomes . . . the one who sent me.' Jesus held up a child because the child symbolized power-lessness, vulnerability and helplessness. Who might he hold up today? A pensioner afraid to step out of her flat for fear of being mugged or assaulted? An asylum-seeker fleeing political oppression or persecution in his homeland? A poor nation desperately trying to secure a fair deal in a global economy hopelessly weighted in favour of the rich? Whoever welcomes such as these, welcomes me.

Who are the people we simply fail to recognize? I believe St Luke's is a welcoming church. But God have mercy on us should we be so caught up with our own internal arguments that we fail to recognize the 'child' in our midst.

But there's another level to consider: are we willing to welcome our own inner child? Whoever welcomes the child within, welcomes the one who created it.

Clearly, there's a world of difference between being child-ish and child-like. When I'm grumpy or irritable because things are not working out, when I disappear in a sulk because I can't get my own way, when I refuse to let that pushy driver get past me, or when I refuse to lose an argument in order to gain a friend, I am behaving like a child in a bad sense – I'm being childish.

None of this is what Jesus meant. What he did mean is up for speculation. He might have been pointing to a child's openness, to its wide-eyed wonder, its playfulness, or its willingness to trust. He might have been calling us to release our sense of control, to admit to what we all know but can't admit to: that inside we sometimes feel lost, helpless, frightened, vulnerable.

I'm sure that one part of being child-like is finding a willingness to dream dreams. What a child-like thing, to dream that one day black people would not be forced to sit at the back of the bus? What a child-like thing, to imagine that women could be priests, that South Africa could have a black president, that the Berlin Wall could be pulled down, that Christians could find a way to disagree constructively, that war might not be the only way? What a child-like thing, to risk all for a dream?

The child within may not have been seen or heard of for years. There may have been very good reasons for hiding him or her away in a deep and hidden place. So I'm not suggesting that it's easy to throw open the gates and embrace your inner child. But I do believe that following Jesus involves being prepared to welcome the child within as well the children without.

Welcome!

———◆———

James 2.1–10, 14–17; Mark 7.24–37

Back in the mid-1970s, I was involved in planting a new church in a little place called Todmorden (in the Calder Valley). Todmorden is a friendly, down-to-earth town on the border between Yorkshire and Lancashire, and the church that emerged reflected the nature of the town – a warm fellowship of good-hearted people.

For some years I used to visit them regularly to preach and advise them on the growth and development of the church. On one visit, ten years or so ago, just as the service began, I noticed a scruffy old woman shuffling in through the doors. Her hair was matted and unkempt, her clothes looked as though they had been scrounged from a dozen bins, and she wafted an unsavoury odour. As she plonked herself on a seat on the front row, everyone stared at her uncomfortably. Halfway through the first hymn the woman, still seated, pulled out a crushed packet of cigarettes and lit up, her exhaled smoke rising into the nostrils of the front rows of worshippers like incense. People looked sideways at each other, wondering what would happen, who would do something.

Eventually, one of the elders stepped towards her, motioning to her to step outside for a chat – which I'm sure he would have done with patience and compassion. However, he wasn't to have the opportunity: as the 'tramp' rose from her seat, she straightened out her stoop, removed her wig and revealed herself as one of the founding members of the church. The local amateur dramatics society (of which she was a keen member) had demonstrated the extraordinary talents of their make-up department – and totally fooled everyone, even lifelong friends of the woman concerned.

However, she wasn't simply testing out the make-up department, or indeed her own acting skills; she cooked up the idea as a way of commenting on the comfortable insularity of the group. Thankfully, they seemed to take it in the right spirit. She had certainly delivered a far more powerful 'sermon' than anything I had travelled 200 miles from London to offer.

Back in Victorian England, William Booth, the founder of the Salvation Army, made a similar point, but in a rather more radical fashion. Booth grew up in Nottingham, where he was converted to Christianity as a young man and became a Methodist. It was less than 50 years since his hero Wesley's death but already some Methodist churches had enshrined themselves in respectability, reserving the best seats for wealthy patrons.

Noticing that few poor people ever attended the Wesley Chapel in the centre of Nottingham, Booth decided to follow Wesley by preaching outdoors, in one of the city's cruellest slums, known appropriately as 'The Bottoms', an area that housed the underclass of the Industrial Revolution.

One Sunday morning in 1846, Booth decided it was time to introduce the congregation at the Chapel to their 'poor relations', who had come to faith through his street preaching. So he led what he called his 'gang of slummers' – ragged and dirty converts from The Bottoms – through the main entrance of the Wesley Chapel, where they filed nervously into the best seats for worship.

The regulars were furious. And Booth's converts were soon banished to using the rear entrance and required to sit on backless wooden benches behind the pulpit, out of sight of the congregation. William Booth was a mere 17 years of age when he marched his converts down the aisle in Nottingham. Just over 20 years later he gave up on the mainstream churches and founded the Salvation Army in the East End of London, concentrating on bringing God's love to the excluded and the downtrodden of his day.

It's amazing how timeless the words of St James appear:

> My brothers and sisters, do you with your acts of favouritism really believe in our glorious Lord Jesus Christ? For if a person with gold rings and in fine clothes comes into your assembly, and if a poor person in dirty clothes also comes in, and if you take notice of the one wearing the fine clothes and say, 'Have a seat here, please', while to the one who is poor you say, 'Stand there', or, 'Sit at my feet', have you not made distinctions among yourselves, and become judges with evil thoughts?

Now the first thing to say is, don't let's beat ourselves up for the wrong reasons. James isn't saying that we can't have favourite people – we all do, and rightly so. And he doesn't expect us to like everyone equally; there are bound to be people we find it hard to like – frankly, some people make it very hard to like them. So don't feel bad about not liking everyone, because that is not the point here.

The point is about exclusion, about prejudice, about people blindness – lumping people together into groups that we don't like, don't want and won't tolerate. It's about judging people, placing them in boxes, refusing to accept them for who they are. And we're not just talking about the economically deprived here: all kinds of people experience prejudice and exclusion.

'But what about Jesus?', you might say. 'What about his treatment of the Syrophoenician woman? Wasn't he being prejudiced against non-Jews?' Well, there are some commentators who suggest that Jesus was being deliberately provocative: that he was drawing out the woman's faith. Well, maybe. But a face-value reading of the story suggests that Jesus stood corrected; that a remarkable woman blasted the limitations of his small-town background. However, the really important thing is that, despite being a Gentile, the woman's daughter was healed. Prejudice did not stand in the way of God's blessing.

I'm quite sure that we at St Luke's have our prejudices and blind spots. But our aspiration is to be an inclusive church – which is probably just a trendy way of saying 'welcoming church'. And I'm very pleased that this is how so many people find St Luke's. But there's no room for complacency. We need continuously to commit ourselves afresh to contribute to the inclusive, welcoming spirit of St Luke's.

Being a welcoming church might mean all kinds of things. At the simplest level, it means being prepared to talk to people you don't know, during or after the service on a Sunday morning. I take it as a sign of spiritual as well as communal health that new people turn up at St Luke's most Sundays. They don't all stay: some are visitors from out of town, some are just taking a peek, some are here for specific reasons, like having their banns read. Whatever their reason for coming, it would be tragic if these people disappeared without anyone talking with them.

Being an inclusive, welcoming church also has to do with the messages we send out to the immediate neighbourhood. Some of this is linked to the attitudes and policies we have as a church – like how we treat people who want to get married here, or who bring their babies for baptism. A couple recently told me that they had asked if their baby daughter could be christened here, some years ago. They were told that she couldn't be christened because they did not attend church. And do you know what? They never did attend church. Who blames them! But just a couple of weeks ago I was privileged to welcome that same little girl into St Luke's to conduct her wedding and to offer the church's blessing (as well as God's) on her and her marriage.

Finally, we are called to the ultimate symbol of God's welcome to us all – the Eucharist, Holy Communion. This is the celebration of divine inclusion, the place where barriers are broken down, the place where all stand on level ground as recipients of divine grace. This is a place of acceptance, not of rejection, a place of love, hope and inclusion. This is the table of Christ. Whoever you are, wherever you come from, whatever your lot in life, whatever your ethnic or racial background, whether you are a man or a woman, straight or gay, whether you earn a pittance or you're worth a fortune, whether you have kids, can't have kids, don't want kids, whether you're full of faith or troubled by doubts, whether you're feeling happy or miserable, hopeful or fearful, gregarious or withdrawn – YOU'RE WELCOME!

Generous spirits

1 Kings 17.10–16; Mark 12.38–44

If I were to ask you to name Jesus' two favourite subjects in the Gospels, what would you say? The first, pretty obviously, is the kingdom of God or the kingdom of heaven; Jesus talked about the kingdom incessantly. But the second is less obvious. Believe it or not, the second most popular theme with Jesus is money.

Actually, the whole Bible is full of references to money. I read somewhere recently that on average, one in eight verses of the Bible in some way talks about money – a statement that ought to give pause for thought to those who seem to think that the most important theme in the Bible is sex!

And the reason for all this preoccupation with money is clear: nothing goes more incisively to the heart of who and what we are as people than the way we earn, spend, share and distribute money.

It's interesting that, in contrast, churches are often shy to talk about money. Once a year we have Gift Day at St Luke's – a Sunday when we make a one-off gift, and review our regular giving towards the life and work of St Luke's. The Bible readings are appropriately both about money, and both about widows, who were among the poorest members of ancient society.

The Gospel reading is one of those well-known passages in the New Testament. The term 'the widow's mite', as a metaphor for sacrificial giving, has transcended religious culture and entered popular consciousness. Just prior to entering the Temple, where the story is set, Jesus warns his listeners about those scribes who, he says, are power- and image-conscious, and who 'devour widows' houses'. It's not entirely clear what he means by devouring widows' houses; but Josephus, the ancient historian, talks about certain Pharisees and scribes who took advantage of vulnerable widows. They apparently solicited the financial support of widows until their money ran out, when they would then move on to the next unsuspecting soul. It was for such people that Jesus reserved his harshest judgement.

In contrast to this is the widow in the story: a non-person, someone apparently invisible to all but Jesus. What she gave was minuscule, a couple of mites, the smallest coins of the day, coins that the wealthy temple-goers would not even bother keeping in their purses. Jesus watched this woman hold out her hand and let go of her entire livelihood. It was an act of utter generosity.

And that's what this story is about: extraordinary generosity. Jesus didn't suggest that everyone should give up their entire living. Not everyone can be a Mother Teresa. The story doesn't offer a blueprint for Christian stewardship; it's a story about spectacular generosity – and the contrast between smug self-righteousness and genuine love of God.

An Oxford student, Lydia Nash, won £16,000 on *Who Wants to be a Millionaire?* She decided to give it all to an orphanage in Thailand. She even abandoned plans to buy a laptop and a new jacket because she realized it would mean much more to the children in Thailand. This is generosity like the widows: beyond the call of duty.

I don't know if Lydia is a Christian – I suspect she is. But you certainly don't have to be a Christian to be generous; some of the most generous people I know never go near a church. God's image is in creation; the divine fingerprints are all over humanity, regardless of whether or not they discover specific faith in Christ.

God is a generous God. The theological-speak for divine generosity is grace. Grace is the overflowing of divine generosity that is felt everywhere, though not necessarily acknowledged. And grace is not to do with merit. It is, as we were always taught, unmerited favour. As Frederick Buechner puts it in *Wishful Thinking*:

> Grace is something you can never get, but only be given. There's no way to earn it or deserve it or bring it about any more than you can deserve the taste of raspberries and cream or earn good looks or bring about your own birth.

A good sleep is grace and so are good dreams. Most tears are grace. The smell of fresh rain is grace. Somebody loving you is grace. Loving somebody is grace. Have you ever *tried* to love somebody?

When we begin to see this, when we recognize the giftedness of life, that everything is an overflowing of a great cosmic generosity, then we feel gratitude. And it is out of that sense of gratitude that we ourselves feel the impulse to be generous. But let me stress that I'm not just talking about money now, I'm talking about a whole generosity of spirit:

- generosity of forgiveness towards those who have wronged us;
- generosity of faith in people;
- generosity with appreciation for what others do for us;
- generosity with compliments and well-wishes;
- generosity with time given to friends and strangers;
- generosity with gifts and talents in the service of those around us.

All these and many other expressions of generosity arise out of a deep sense of gratitude for the grace we ourselves have received.

So it's perfectly natural that generous giving is part of our worship. It's right and proper that we suddenly pass hats around and turn our attention to such mundane stuff as money. It's a response of gratitude for the given-ness of life itself. But let no one talk about it as a whip-round, or a donation to the work of the church. It's worship. It's an act of gratitude and thanksgiving to the one who is the fount of all generosity.

The difference between the widow and the wealthy donors at the temple treasury was gratitude. She had so little, yet she felt that she possessed everything that mattered. The others had so much, yet they never felt that they had enough.

To get to the nub of what I am saying: community is a place that is created by generosity. Just look at our world. Here in the West we have never been so wealthy, yet we have never been so fragmented. Social cohesion has never been so poor. A society based on selfishness and personal acquisitiveness can never experience real community. A society can be no wider, deeper or stronger than the quantity of gratitude its members share with each other and with those beyond.

The church should above all else be a household of generosity, a community where grace abounds. Historically the Church of England has been such a place, a home for generous spirits; I pray it will not now fall into the hands of niggardly souls who know little of grace or gratitude.

I believe a generous spirit is growing among us here. God preserve it. God save us from the elitism of being 'cool'. God keep us from mean, ungenerous attitudes towards each other. God keep us open, uncynical, caring, forgiving, willing to work for the common good, ready to embrace those we don't yet know. God keep us grateful. God keep us child-like. God fill us with his generous Spirit.

The living word

1 Timothy 3.14—4.5; John 5.36b–47

In an earlier reflection I included some excerpts from the little book *Children's Letters to God*. Here are a few more:

> Dear God, OK I kept my half of the deal. Where's the bike?

> Dear God, how did you know you were God?

> Dear God, I know you are supposed to love thy neighbour, but if Mark keeps taking my other skate he's going to get it.

And there's one letter that is particularly poignant. It reads:

> Dear God, I think the Bible is very good. But did you write any other books?

It's not a bad a question. I mean, you would think God would be a bit more prolific, wouldn't you? And let's face it: we've all wished we could lay our hands on those other books – the ones that prove unambiguously that we are on the right side of the argument, and the other lot are wrong!

But for better or worse, there's just the one book – and like it or not, it doesn't always say what we want it to.

There have been great arguments recently about homosexuality. It doesn't seem that long ago that similar rows raged about women priests. During the mid-1980s I was a minister in a quite conservative part of the Church. The idea of having women on an equal footing with men in church leadership was unthinkable. And of course much of the argument revolved around the Bible. The twelve disciples of Jesus were men, it was argued (needless to say, it was overlooked that they were also all Jews). And then there were the letters of St Paul, which seemed to advocate female subordination in the home as well as in the Church. All of this was taken very seriously in the churches where I worked.

But the more I thought about it, the more preposterous it seemed that in this day and age leaders or priests should have to be men. In biblical times, women were largely uneducated and treated as little more than male possessions in a patriarchal culture. But why should this have any bearing on the sort of roles and jobs that women perform today, when it's patently obvious that women can do most jobs as well if not better than men?

Well, it all seems fairly obvious now, but at the time lots of people were very angry with me for arguing in that way. It became common for people to stand up and heckle me on the subject, accusing me of swapping the word of God for trendy, secular feminist ideas. Actually, I seem to have been dogged by these sorts of people. A couple of years ago, when I was speaking at the Australian equivalent of Greenbelt in Sydney, a man came to all my seminars and shouted me down every time, accusing me of throwing the Bible away. The stupid thing is, if we were to have a test to see who reads the Bible most, I know who would win. Lots of these zealous defenders of the Bible are really arguing for what they want the Bible to say rather than what it does say.

The fact is, the Bible is very important to me. I grew up in a church that gave me a deep respect – and love – for scripture, and a biblical knowledge that has served me well throughout my career as a minister. That's not to say that I don't have problems with the Bible: I certainly do. At times I love it, other times it frustrates me and angers me; sometimes it feeds my soul as well as my mind, other times I want to toss it in the bin.

But the Bible remains central to my faith. I read it nearly every day of my life, I'm intrigued by its strange world, I love the cleverly woven literature of the Old Testament, and I can't easily disregard what I think it says. A few years ago I studied for a Masters degree in Biblical Interpretation – which both deepened my love of the text and sharpened my critical skills as a reader. And I am passionate to teach the Bible and debate its meaning for us today with anyone who will give me a hearing.

So the attitude from some who stand on the conservative side of debates about women's ordination, women bishops, gay relationships and the like, that the rest of us are woolly liberals who just disregard scripture, is, frankly, rubbish. The issue can't be reduced to a division between those who are biblical and those who aren't. It's much more a matter of what models of biblical interpretation you choose to use.

One of the things that attracted me to the Anglican Church is its generous openness to different points of view; it is a family of many traditions. And I like the wonderful breadth that it shows in the task of discerning the mind of God. Let me explain a bit about that.

Back in the sixteenth century, when the Church of England was still finding its feet, a guy called Richard Hooker penned the first piece of systematic Anglican writing in a highly significant book with the snappy title *On the Laws of Ecclesiastical Polity*. One of his famous passages is the guideline for Anglican thinking that maintains that truth should be sought by consulting and balancing the testimonies of scripture, tradition and reason. All three are vital to Hooker, and none of them could be understood apart from the other two. It's called Hooker's three-legged stool.

At the Lambeth Conference in 1988, the worldwide assembly of Anglican bishops added a fourth leg to the stool – human experience. The bishops thought that the experience of Christians living today was also needed in the task of discerning the mind of God.

Of course, it's ironic that so recently as 1988 the bishops should affirm the importance of the experience of present-day Christians in the search for truth, when in the current argument the experience of godly gay clergy and lay people is being sidelined by some of those very same bishops in favour of dogmatic and selective readings of the Bible. Bring back Hooker's three-legged stool, I say.

In the Gospel reading, Jesus takes the Jewish leaders to task on a similar point. 'You study the scriptures diligently', he says, 'supposing that in having them you have eternal life . . . yet you refuse to come to me for that life' (New English Bible). Basically he was saying, 'You're completely missing the point. In your zeal to dissect every jot and tittle of the text you're failing to get hold of the spirit of the whole thing.'

His point is underlined earlier in the chapter. He heals a man on the Sabbath who has been crippled for 38 years. Surely this is what real religion is all about – doing good for people, caring about those on the margins. But the religious leaders miss that point altogether; instead they come down like a ton of bricks on the poor man who was healed because he is carrying his bed on the Sabbath in contradiction to the law of Moses. Fundamentalists are not a new invention!

Paul says something along the same lines in his second letter to the Corinthians: 'The letter kills, but the Spirit gives life.'

Perhaps he was thinking about another massive argument that almost split the early church, just as homosexuality is doing today. Less than 20 years after the death of Jesus, Jews were sitting down to eat with pagans. It was outrageous, and the apostles at Jerusalem called a gathering of the Primates to discuss it! Despite it being against the law of Moses, and unbiblical, Paul defended the new inclusiveness. It did contravene Mosaic law, but represented perfectly the true spirit of what the Bible is all about.

Paul pioneered an approach to the Bible which also applies to his own words in the New Testament. We should not concentrate on the letter of the text but try to get at the underlying point of scripture. If Paul and Peter and others had kept strictly to the letter of the Old Testament there would be no Church as we know it today. They recognized that the Holy Spirit – the spirit of scripture – was still working and revealing new things. And the evidence for this lay in the experiences of those who loved God and tried to do his will. The application of this in present-day debates is all too obvious.

So is it worth reading the Bible? Does it have anything to offer us today? Absolutely. Scripture is important, not least because it offers us precious insights into the faith of two communities – the early Church and the ancient people of Israel. And as we follow the lectionary readings week in, week out, we hear the great record of God's action in history and its impact on men and women rehearsed again and again. In so doing we internalize that history and make it part of our own experience.

I don't read the Bible for clear and unambiguous directions on the issues of twenty-first-century life. It isn't a manual that gives us step-by-step instructions on tricky subjects like sexuality, divorce, computers that keep crashing or how to bring up your kids. It's as much a set of questions posed to the Church as a set of answers. Those people who imagine that the Bible is a means of resolving moral dilemmas or an unambiguous code for proper behaviour clearly only read certain bits of it, and attribute to it an absolute, unchanging quality (alien to its own testimony) that denies freedom to God and that denies our own historical responsibility.

The American biblical scholar, Walter Brueggemann, had this to say:

The Bible finally is not concerned with right morality, right piety, or right doctrine. Rather it is concerned with faithful relationships between God and the people, between all the brothers and sisters in God's community and the world God has made. Faithful relationships of course can never be reduced to formulae but live always in the free, risking exchange that is the very nature of genuine relationship. It is this kind of exchange rather than fixed absolutes that is the stuff of biblical faith.

That'll do for me.

The communion of saints

Hebrews 11.32—12.2; John 11.32–44

There was a marvellous poignancy in celebrating the feast of All Saints on the day of my friend Mike Yaconelli's funeral. He was an inspiration to countless thousands of people here in this country, in the USA and around the world. It was sad to think that this bearded, hilarious, spiritual liberator would no longer hold us under his spell. But Mike was a saint indeed, and there was no more fitting day to bid him farewell.

Autumn is a gloriously dismal time of year. It's a season of huge change. Hot summer days drift into the distance as chilly winds whistle through the trees, and short-sleeved shirts give way to woolly sweaters; clocks change in a rite of passage to the darker, colder days that lie ahead.

And there's a change of tone in the passage of the church year too. The long months of Trinity come to an end, and we begin the countdown to Advent and Christmas once again. And here we pass through a short season that draws our attention to human mortality and the hope of life beyond this world. The ancient feasts of All Saints and All Souls are placed alongside the more recent addition of Remembrance Day.

I confess to mixed feelings about this time of year. I love the autumn, and I do find something satisfying about the way in which the Christian vision of death meshes into the descent of nature during these months. But I don't too much enjoy the reminders of my own mortality; the realization that my flesh, like the rest, is but as grass.

This probably says something about my own personality, but it also reveals how much I am a part of our wider culture that hates to deal with issues surrounding death. Ours is a consumerist culture, preoccupied with wanting, acquiring and possessing – as if having lots of things will shield us from the inevitability of growing old and dying. Sadly, there's often little room for longing, yearning and wondering, the stuff of mystery and the peculiar unknown.

As a parish priest who conducts around 40 funerals each year, I am able more than most to observe people dealing with the loss of loved ones. All too often they bathe themselves in sentimentality – almost trying to pretend that this isn't really death. One of the most popular readings people request is Henry Scott Holland's poem, which opens with the words: 'Death is nothing at all: I have only slipped away into the next room.' But that's not really true, is it? Death is something; it's something devastating. And our loved ones aren't really in the next room. In the end we have to get beyond the sentiment and face the fact that a hole now exists in our life.

Dietrich Bonhoeffer, the Christian theologian executed by the Nazis, had plenty of time to contemplate death in his prison cell. In one of his famous letters from prison he wrote:

Nothing can make up for the absence of someone we love . . . it is nonsense to say that God fills the gap; God doesn't fill it, but on the contrary, God keeps it empty and so helps us keep alive our former communion with each other, even at the cost of pain . . . the dearer and richer the memories, the more difficult the separation. But gratitude changes the pangs of memory into tranquil joy. The beauties of the past are borne, not as a thorn in the flesh, but as a precious gift in themselves.

The wisdom of Bonhoeffer's words sweep aside both cheap sentimentality and high-minded super-spirituality. We don't have to recover from the death of a loved one. There is a gap in our lives that may never be filled. The Christian hope is not asking us to pretend that death hasn't happened – it is reminding us that the pain we carry will some day turn into gratitude, joy and wonder.

And I don't believe it is just those of us who are left behind who struggle to let go of those we love; I'm of the opinion that the departed also experience bereavement. Of course there's no way of being sure about such things, but it's an idea that C. S. Lewis apparently held as well. Indeed, he even toyed with the thought that the fairly common 'visitations' some people experience from their loved ones in the days following their departure are part of a grieving process, both for the departed and for those left behind.

Bonhoeffer's reference to communion across the divide of death is crucial in all of this, because at the heart of a Christian understanding of death lies the notion of the communion of saints. If you are an Anglican you have probably affirmed your faith in this a thousand times: 'I believe in the holy Catholic Church: the communion of saints', etc.

The first thing to say about this is that 'saints' here does not simply refer to the good and the great, but to the whole family of those who are embraced in God's love. All Saints' Day could be thought of as a family reunion. At this party there are heroes and scoundrels, beloved aunts and estranged cousins, relatives we adore and those who plainly baffle us. They are all ours, and we are included.

Gathering around the eucharistic table, we worship amid a great fluttering of wings, with the whole host of heaven crowding the air above our heads. Luke is there, Thomas the doubter is there, the Virgin Mary, Mother Teresa – and Mike Yaconelli! But there are also all those we have person- ally loved and lost – call their names and hear them answer 'Present'. All Saints' Day could be seen as a great family reunion.

I believe in the communion of saints. I believe we are embedded in a community of souls who support and guide us – those we see and know, and a vast cloud of others who are invisible yet present. We live in a community in time and space, but we also live within the great body of human mem- ory. Those who lived centuries ago touch our lives, and we hope our lives will mean something to those who haven't yet been born.

I believe in the communion of saints, a community that spans cultures, social class, gender, sexuality, living and dead. 'For all the saints' includes me and goes beyond and before me. Somehow I am a part of this great memory and hope of God's all-inclusive love, which goes beyond time and even death, encompassing today and stretching into the vast future of a world still to come.

There's a film that captures the spirit of the communion of saints perfectly; it's a 1980s Robert Benton production called *Places in the Heart*. It's set during the Great Depression in Texas. Edna Spalding (played by Sally Field) is left a widow after her husband is accidentally shot by a drunk. A mother of two, she battles to avoid the family farm being repossessed by the bank. In desperation she decides to plant a cotton crop, despite having no experience in cotton growing. For- tune brings a runaway slave into Edna's life, a man who knows everything there is to know about growing cotton. And she also takes on a blind boarder (John Malkovich), and this rather odd little community slowly begins to turn the sit- uation around.

The last scene is a Sunday morning communion service at church. The communion bread and cup are passed down the pews of the church. And suddenly the camera begins to show the faces of those who have come to church that morning. The slave who has run away is sitting next to a Klansman. The town banker, who has no mercy, receives communion from the dead husband who is also present. The blind man passes the plate to an old woman he cannot see, and a lonely husband takes the cup from a strong, brave child. In this magical, mysterious scene, those living and dead, young and old, of value and devalued, worthy and worthless, are gathered together in peace and union to receive the body and blood of Christ.

Every time we celebrate the Eucharist, we are surrounded by mums and dads, grandmas and granddads, brothers and sisters, dear friends and partners who are no longer with us in the flesh. We are linked to people around the world whom we don't know and may never meet. We embrace those who have gone before with those who are not yet born. I believe in the communion of saints.

The communion of saints is a living, moving, breathing organism, reaching beyond time and place, holding all of eternity in a sacred moment. And we can know it. We can know that we are a part of it.

One of the great themes of the twenty-first century is connectedness: ecological science explores the complex patterns that knit together the vast diversity of life on planet Earth. Christians affirm that the underlying pattern is love, indeed that love is the thread that stitches the entire universe together and creates relationships that live beyond time and space.

I believe in the communion of saints. I believe in a love stronger than death, that creates and sustains that community. I believe in an ultimate interconnectedness that even the grave cannot destroy. I believe in the God who unites all things in his own being. I believe that in the Eucharist we enter afresh the divine mystery. I believe in God. I believe in the wisdom of eternal love. I believe in life. I believe in fellowship. I believe in the communion of saints.

Christi the King

Revelation 1.4b–8; John 18.33–37

It seems odd to say that the festival of Christ the King is the last Sunday of the year, but of course, the Christian calendar differs from the usual one. Advent Sunday, which follows, is the beginning of the church year, and we start the whole story all over again as we prepare for Christmas and the coming of the Christ child. The festival of Christ the King is the point at which we contemplate what we mean by God's kingdom, and what sort of king we see Jesus to be.

In today's world the notion of Christ's kingship is deeply contested in some quarters – and not without justification. After all, we now have the benefit of history. To be sure, the Church began as a vulnerable and relatively insignificant body of people who were mercilessly persecuted within the Roman Empire. But it didn't stay that way. After Constantine made Christianity the established religion in the Empire, the Church became a powerful institution and Christ's kingship became a cipher for all kinds of power-hungry people to inflict bloodshed and persecution on others in his name.

The Crusades are a good example of this. Not for the first or the last time, certain kings opted for conflict on foreign soil as a way of boosting popularity at home. The upshot was a bloody conflict with Muslims in the Middle East, the spectre of which still haunts us today.

Against this background, some theologians warn against

monarchical models of the divine. Sallie McFague, for example, offers a reconstructed vision of God that replaces the traditional models of God as King and Father with God as Mother, Lover and Friend.

I have a lot of sympathy with her approach, and I readily take the images of God as Mother, Lover and Friend into my own spirituality. But do we really have to abandon the notion of Christ's kingship altogether? I don't think so – because Jesus completely redefines the nature of kingship in his teaching about the kingdom of God.

False notions of Christ's kingship – images of a tribal monarch who leads his people into battle, smiting their enemies and conquering all before them – have nothing to do with the kingdom Jesus preached. Admittedly, this is the picture we find in much of the Old Testament, but Jesus represents a thorough paradigm shift where kingship is concerned.

The Bible passage from John says it all. Here in this courtroom drama Jesus tells Pilate that his kingdom is not of this world. If it were, he says, his followers would be fighting on his behalf. But that's not what his kingship is about. Here we have a shepherd-king, one not afraid to make himself vulnerable, who is willing to make the supreme sacrifice for his people, who is not interested in creating followers through violence or coercion, or who plays politics at others' expense. This is a king who does not seek an eye for an eye or a tooth for a tooth. His kingdom is based on love and compassion, on peace and goodwill, on justice and integrity, on child-like openness and playfulness, on opportunities to change and a willingness to forgive.

This king is still around today. He likes to go out into the streets in disguise. He turns up as a street person, a homeless, battered woman, a black teen being taunted by racists, and whispers to us that as we care for everyone, we care for him. As we care for him, we learn what loving sacrifice means.

When we are humble enough to learn how to serve, we are able to recognize Christ as king.

This is kingship. But it's a different sort of kingship. It's kingship that has experienced a paradigm shift, a quantum leap in a different direction.

The American columnist Sydney Harris tells a story about a Quaker friend whom he one day accompanied to a newsstand. The friend greeted the man behind the counter very courteously, but in return he received a gruff and rude response. Accepting the newspaper that was shoved roughly in his direction, Harris's friend politely smiled and wished the newsman a nice weekend. As the two friends walked down the street, the columnist asked: 'Does he always treat you so rudely?'

'Yes, unfortunately he does.'

'And are you always so polite and friendly to him?'

'Yes, I am.'

'Why are you so nice to him when he is so unfriendly to you?', Harris asked. To which his friend replied: 'Because I don't want him to decide how I'm going to act. Why should I let *him* decide how *I'm* going to act?'

That, in a very elemental way, is the kingdom of God Jesus taught. It's about learning to act rather than simply react, to live by a different principle.

The Jewish psychiatrist Viktor Frankl gives a similar example of this from his days in concentration camps during the war:

Those of us who were there can remember the people who walked through the huts comforting others, giving away their last piece of bread. They may have been few in number, but they offer sufficient proof that everything can be taken from a person but one thing: the last of human freedoms – to choose one's attitude in any set of circumstances, to choose one's own way. And there were always choices to make. Every day, every hour, offered the opportunity to make a decision, a decision which determined whether or not you become the plaything of circumstance, renouncing freedom and dignity to become moulded into the form of a typical inmate.

It may be odd to think of a concentration-camp inmate as a king, but Frankl's description is of people who were living out God's kingdom even in the most oppressive circumstances. Like Jesus, they refused to be playthings; they 'ruled' over their circumstances – and over the evil being inflicted upon them – rather than being ruled by them. They experienced a paradigm shift into a whole new framework of reference. In one sense it's an unnatural way of looking at things; but within Christ's kingdom paradigm, it's absolutely natural.

Both these stories point us to a crucial truth: that the kingdom of God is not an external thing; it's not a geographical location or an organization that you join – it's within us. Whether faced with the appalling surroundings of a concentration camp, or just dealing with the frustrations and unkindness of people in everyday life, we walk Christ's kingly way when we draw on the deep resources of his kingdom within our own beings.

Let me end with a meditation along these lines from *The Clown in the Belfry* by Frederick Buechner:

If only we had eyes to see and ears to hear and wits to understand, we would know that the kingdom of God in the sense of holiness, goodness, and beauty is as close as breathing and is crying out to be born within ourselves and within the world; we would know that the kingdom of God is what we all of us long for above all things even when we don't know its name or realize that it's what we're starving to death for.

The kingdom of God is where our best dreams come

from, our truest prayers. We glimpse it at those moments when we find ourselves being better than we are, and wiser than we know. We catch sight of it when at some moment of crisis a strength seems to come to us that is greater than our strength.

The kingdom of God is where we belong. It is home, and whether we realize it or not, I think we are all of us homesick for it.

Jesus said, 'The kingdom of God is among you.'

Anthony Bloom says that if we cannot meet God within, in the very depth of ourselves, our chances of meeting him outside ourselves are very remote. If we cannot find a contact with God under our own skin, as it were, then the chances are very slight that we will recognize him outside, even if we meet him face to face. St John Chrysostom said, 'Find the door of your heart, and you will discover it as the door of the kingdom of God.'

I believe in the kingdom of God. I believe it's all around – in the love of friends and strangers, in the beauty of nature, in the playfulness of a dog or cat, in the resilience of those who resist evil and prejudice, in the hope of a more just world, in the will to do better, in the gift of imagination, in the prayers of people who care. I believe it's buried in our own hearts like a treasure in a field waiting to be discovered. I believe in Jesus. I believe in this sort of king.

References

Betjeman, John, 'Christmas', *Collected Poems*, London: John Murray, 2003.

Bloom, Anthony, *School of Prayer*, London: Darton, Longman and Todd, 1970

Blue, Lionel, *Bolts from the Blue*, London: Hodder & Stoughton, 1986.

Bonhoeffer, Dietrich, *Letters and Papers from Prison*, London: SCM Press, 1993.

Brueggemann, Walter, *The Prophetic Imagination*, London: SCM Press, 1978.

Buechner, Frederick, *The Clown in the Belfry*, San Francisco, CA: HarperCollins, 1992.

Buechner, Frederick, *Listening to Your Life: Daily Meditations*, San Francisco, CA: HarperCollins, 1992.

Buechner, Frederick, *Whistling in the Dark*, San Francisco, CA: HarperCollins, 1993.

Buechner, Frederick, *Wishful Thinking: A Seeker's ABC*, San Francisco, CA: HarperCollins, 1993.

Children's Letters to God, compiled by Eric Marshall and Stuart Hample, London: Fount, 1975.

Frankl, Viktor, quoted in Jonathan Magonet, *A Rabbi's Bible*, London: SCM Press, 1991.

Gerrish, Brian, *The Pilgrim Road*, Louisville, KY: Westminster John Knox Press, 2000.

Gordon, Mary, *Final Payments*, New York: Ballantine Books, 1994.

Harris, Sydney, quoted in Brian Gerrish, *The Pilgrim Road*, Louisville, KY: Westminster John Knox Press, 2000.

Hughes, Gerard, *God of Surprises*, London: Darton, Longman and Todd, 1996.

Kushner, Harold, *The Lord is My Shepherd: The Healing Wisdom of the Twenty-third Psalm*, London, Hodder & Stoughton, 2003.

L'Engle, Madeleine, *And it was Good: Reflections on Beginnings*, Wheaton, IL: Harold Shaw Publishers, 1983.

McNamara, William, *Mystical Passion: The Art of Christian Loving*, Shaftesbury, Dorset: Element Books, 1994.

McNamara, William, *The Human Adventure: The Art of Contemplating Living*, Shaftesbury, Dorset: Element Books, 1994.

Macquarrie, John, *Jesus in Modern Thought*, London: SCM Press, 1990.

Milne, A. A., *The House at Pooh Corner*, London: Egmont Books, 2004.

Nouwen, Henri, *Bread for the Journey: Reflections for Every Day of the Year*, London: Darton, Longman and Todd, 1996.

Rilke, Rainer Maria, *Letters to a Young Poet*, New York: Random House, 2001.

Studdert Kennedy, G. A., *The Word and the Work*, London: Longmans, 1925.

Thielicke, Helmut, *How Modern Should Theology Be?*, Philadelphia, PA: Fortress Press, 1970.

Tyler, Anne, *The Clock Winder*, New York: Vintage Books, 1987.